INTIMACY WITH GOD

INTIMACY WITH GOD

by Richard Booker
author of *The Miracle of the Scarlet Thread*
and *Come and Dine*

Foreword by Tim LaHaye

Bridge Publishing, Inc.
Publishers of:
LOGOS • HAVEN • OPEN SCROLL

Scriptural quotations have been carefully selected from the following versions of the Bible:

The New King James Bible, copyright © 1979, 1980, 1982, Thomas Nelson, Inc., Nashville, TN (NKJ)

New International Version, copyright © New York International Bible Society. Used by permission (NIV)

Revised Standard Version, copyright © 1946, 1952, 1971, 1973 (RSV)

INTIMACY WITH GOD

Printed and bound in Great Britain by
Forsyth Middleton & Co. Ltd.
Library of Congress Catalog Card Number: 84-70055
International Standard Book Number: 0-88270-552-0
Bridge Publishing Inc., South Plainfield,
New Jersey 07080
Valley Books, Gwent, U.K.

Contents

Foreword

A person's attitude toward God will affect the way he looks at almost everything in life; himself, sin, eternity and even other people. Your attitude toward God is influenced primarily by your knowledge of Him as He is revealed in the Bible.

Among the many books in the average Christian bookstore today, few will be found about God himself. Many have been written about man, his feelings, self-acceptance and his family, but few about God. One reason is the heavy treatment this important subject is given by most Bible scholars. Many use such long and ponderous titles for God, the average layman cannot understand them.

Much in the Bible was written to tell us about God, His nature and His interest in mankind. It should be simple, understandable and reassuring. And that is just what this book is. It is biblical and detailed, but understandable. *Intimacy With God* will warm your heart as it gives you a true picture of your loving heavenly Father who was omnipotent enough to create everything that is to be found on earth, in heaven and in the universe but who was also loving enough to send His only begotten Son to die personally for your sins. The Bible reveals such a God in its library of sixty-six books: you need to know Him.

Richard Booker is to be commended for putting together those Scriptures that teach about God and for presenting us a composite and easily understood picture of Him in this one volume. Reading this book will enrich and deepen your life because it will give you a complete portrait of your heavenly Father.

Dr. Tim LaHaye
Author, Educator, Minister
President, Family Life Seminars

About the Author

Richard Booker is an author and Bible teacher presently living in Houston, Texas. His organization, Sounds of the Trumpet, Inc., provides Christian teachings through books, tapes, workshops, etc. Prior to his call to the teaching ministry, Richard was a computer and management consultant, climbing the corporate career ladder. His B.S. and M.B.A. degrees well prepared him. His career became his god, and he spent ten years chasing that elusive idol, dragging his wife, Peggy, across the country with him.

During that time he lectured throughout the United States, Canada and Mexico, training over one thousand management and computer personnel. His more than twenty articles appeared in the leading computer publications. He was listed in *Who's Who in Computers and Automation, Who's Who in Training and Development,* and *The Dictionary of International Biography,* and was a frequent speaker for the American Management Association.

In the middle 1970s, God gave Richard an "Emmaus Road" experience that changed his life. He left his career to devote all his time to writing and teaching about God's Word. He is the author of several books, articles for Christian magazines and other works.

In addition to his Bible classes and teaching tapes, Richard developed and teaches a one-day workshop on how to study the Bible. A list of his Bible study materials is included at the back of this book.

1

Introduction

In many parts of the world today, people are told that there is no God. Religion is considered to be the "opiate of the masses" which numbs their minds to reality. This is the official party line of communist countries where the state is actually worshiped as God. Non-communist countries express a belief in God. Yet, in these countries, there are some individuals who profess to be *atheist,* one who denies the existence of God. Others claim to be *agnostic,* one who is not sure if God exists or does not exist. And then others who do believe that God exists are *deist,* one who believes that there is a God but that God is neither "knowable," nor active in the affairs of men. And then there are *seekers,* those who believe in God and desire to know Him but do not know where or how to find Him. Seekers know about God, but they don't know Him. Therefore, they have various false ideas of what God is like. Finally, there are *believers,* those who know God and desire to know Him better.

1

Why I Wrote This Book

Everyone is either an atheist, agnostic, deist, seeker or believer. *Which are you?* However you answer that question, this book is for you. I wrote it just for you. If you are an atheist or an agnostic, you can know there is a living God. If you are a deist, you can come to know God and find comfort in His sovereign activity in the affairs of men. If you are a seeker, you can find God and have a correct understanding of Who He is and how you can fellowship with Him. And for the believer, I pray that this book will help you to know Him even better and raise your consciousness of just how great and glorious is our God.

A Look at What's Ahead

You will begin in Part One by discovering the *personality* of God. You will find the answer to the question, "Does God really exist?" Yes, you can know without any doubts. God has given us clear and abundant witnesses to His existence. We will see what they are and then begin to look into the very heart of God so that we might understand Who He is and how we can know Him.

Then, in Part Two, you'll begin to discover what God is like. You'll learn about His *majestic attributes.* An attribute is a truth that God has revealed about Himself. They are revelations of what God is like in His very essence and being. God's majestic attributes reveal to us that God is sovereign, all-knowing, all-powerful, everywhere present and unchanging in all that He is in Himself. I call these God's majestic attributes because they reveal the greatness of God.

Finally, in Part Three, you'll examine God's *moral attributes.* These are revelations of what God is like in His character. God's moral attributes reveal to us that God, in His character, is perfectly holy, perfectly loving, perfectly just and perfectly good.

Well, you can see right off that God is not like us. He is different from all His creatures. This is why we all need to know Him. I pray that God will use this book to give you a personal revelation of Who He is and His plans and purposes

2

for your life so that you may have *Intimacy With God.*

An Appendix is included in the back of the book which provides Scripture references for the different attributes of God. To become more intimate with God, you should look up these references, write them down in the space provided and meditate on them.

In addition, there is a Scripture Index included after the Appendix. The Scripture Index lists every Scripture mentioned in this book and the page number where it is found.

PART 1
GOD'S PERSONALITY

2
Knowing God

If there really is a God, He exists for Himself. By this, I mean that God does not need anything or anybody. His delight is in Himself simply because there is nothing or no one higher than Himself in which to delight. Because He is God, He is sufficient in Himself and in need of nothing. So if God chose to create something, He would be under no obligation to reveal Himself to that which He has created.

It's Up to God

But suppose God did create something? Suppose God created humans? And suppose God chose to reveal Himself to His human creatures. *If God chose to reveal Himself to us, He would have to take the initiative to make Himself known.*

This, of course, is the way it is with people. You can only know someone if they will let you know them. But, if they won't let you get close to them and really know them, then the best you can do is only know about them. And the further a person is removed from us, the more difficult it becomes to know them. So the higher position in life a person has, the more it becomes that person's initiative to make himself known, if he is to be known. Doesn't that make sense? Good!

A Presidential Example

Let me give you an example. The presidency of the United States is the highest office in the land. Because of his position, the president is not available to the average citizen. You can't just walk up to the White House and say, "Can the president come out and play?" If you are to know the president of the United States, he must take the initiative.

President Carter was a good example of a president who took some initiative so that the average citizen could know him. He conducted town meetings in different cities around the country. He would go to a particular town and hold a meeting where the average citizens of that town could come and meet him. After the meeting was over, he would go and spend the evening at the house of a local family. They would talk about things that were near and dear to each other, so that the family got to know the president. But it was the president's initiative that made it possible. They would not have known him if he had not taken the initiative. Now this family may have had a lot of money. They may have been well educated. They may have had a lot of power and prestige in the community. But from then on, the thing they talked about for the rest of their lives was that they "know the president."

God's Initiative

In a similar way, God has taken the initiative to reveal Himself to us. He has done so because He wants us to know Him. Many people don't realize that God wants us to know Him. They don't even think they can know Him. So now we ask the question, *Can we know God?* The answer is yes!

But let's let God speak for Himself. We find Him speaking the following words through the Prophet Jeremiah, "Thus says the LORD: 'Let not the wise man glory in his wisdom, let not the mighty man glory in his might, let not the rich man glory in his riches; but let him who glories glory in this, that he understands and knows Me, that I am the LORD who practice steadfast love, justice, and righteousness in the earth; for in these things I delight, says the LORD'" (Jeremiah 9:23-24 RSV).

Yes, God says He wants us to know Him. *Knowing God means to have intimate spiritual union and communion with Him as a husband and wife know each other.* When you come to know God in this way, He will be the only thing you will talk about for the rest of your life. You won't glory in your riches, or your education, or your power and prestige. You won't glory in yourself or the things of the world. You will glory in knowing Him.

How God Makes Himself Known

So now we see that God wants us to know Him in a very personal way. We have also learned that, if we are to know Him, He must take the initiative. Well, I've got some good news for you! God has taken the initiative. God has revealed Himself to us in four ways, about which we are now going to learn.

God's Revelation in Creation

The first way in which God has revealed Himself to us is through His *creative order.* All we have to do to realize there is a God is to open our eyes and look at His creation. Have you ever wondered how the snow knows just when to fall? How the rain knows just when to drop? How the clouds know just when to open up? How the sun knows just when to rise and set? How the moon knows just when to shine? How the tide knows when it is supposed to be high and when it's supposed to be low? How the seasons know just when to change? How it is that all of creation, except man, functions with perfect order and harmony?

9

Well, the answer, of course, is that there is a God in heaven Who has created all things. And He is a God of order. His creative order testifies to His existence. King David, the sweet Psalmist of Israel, said it this way, "The heavens declare the glory of God; and the firmament shows His handiwork" (Psalms 19:1 NKJ).

A thousand years later, another Jew by the name of Paul said, "For since the creation of the world God's invisible qualities—his eternal power and divine nature—have been clearly seen, being understood from what has been made, so that men are without excuse" (Romans 1:20 NIV).

An Honest Scientist

Sir Isaac Newton was a brilliant English scientist. He had made a miniature model of the solar system which he kept in his home. Right in the middle was a large golden ball representing the sun. Smaller balls representing the planets revolved around it. These all operated harmoniously and were kept in proper orbit, by means of rods and wheels and belts all working together.

One day a friend called on Sir Isaac. Now it happens that the friend did not believe there was a God Who created the universe. But when he saw the miniature model of the solar system and how it all worked together in perfect harmony, he said, "Newton, what a fantastic model of the solar system. Who made it?" Now Sir Isaac was a bit of a tease. And to show his friend how foolish was his disbelief, he responded with a serious tone, "Oh, nobody made it. I just got up one morning and here it was in the study. All the balls and cogs, and belts, and gears just happened to come together. And then, wonder of wonders, they all began revolving in their exact orbits with perfect timing." His friend got the point. *Do you?*

God's Revelation in Instinct

The second way in which God has revealed Himself to us is through *instinct*. We call it our conscience. All of us have a built-in God-consciousness. No matter how far away we may be from God, we still know that He is around. Our conscience, regardless of how hardened it may be, constantly reminds us that there is a God in heaven Who created us in His image.

But what does it mean to be created in God's image? It means that we are spiritual and moral beings. God has created us with a sense of right and wrong so that we make moral judgments. We may not do right and our understanding of what is right may be blurred. But we know we ought to do right. You who are reading this book know you ought to do right. But who told you that you should do right? Well, nobody told you. You just know. But how do you know? You know because there is a God in heaven who delights in doing right and He has put this same sense of right and wrong within each of us. The result is that we make moral judgments. The further we get away from God, the less right are the judgments we make. But we still know we should make them.

Now let's see how the Apostle Paul says this. Romans 1:18-19 reads, "The wrath of God is being revealed from heaven against all the godlessness and wickedness of men who suppress the truth by their wickedness, since what may be known about God is plain to them, because God has made it plain to them" (NIV).

The Apostle Paul says it again in Romans 2:14-15, "Indeed, when Gentiles, who do not have the law, do by nature things required by the law, they are a law for themselves, even though they do not have the law, since they show that the requirements of the law are written on their hearts, their consciences also bearing witness, and their thoughts now accusing, now even defending them" (NIV).

Because of God's witness to Himself through creation and instinct, the Bible never attempts to prove God's existence. It assumes His existence and simply states that anyone who thinks otherwise is a fool (Psalms 53:1).

A Curious Native

There is only one problem with God's revelations of Himself through creation and instinct. They are incomplete.

11

They only help us to *know about God.* It's like if a native on some remote island found a watch that drifted ashore. He can observe that watch and see that there is some kind of order to the watch. He would know that someone "way out there somewhere beyond the vastness of the ocean" made that watch. He would probably begin to wonder about the person who made it. He would form mental images of what this person is like. But most of what he pictured in his mind about the watchmaker would not be right. In other words, the native cannot know the watchmaker just by having the watch. He will remain ignorant of the one who made it.

But suppose, as he examines the watch, he notices a small piece of paper with some writing on it. It says, "This watch was made by 'So-and-So,' whose family has been making watches for the past one hundred years. His picture is enclosed. 'So-and-So' takes great pride in his craftsmanship and personally inspects each watch before pronouncing it good. To keep it in working order, read the following instructions."

Well, with this extra bit of information, the native can begin to know the one who made the watch. He's got something in writing about the watchmaker, in addition to his picture. Now when he wears the watch and thinks of the one who made it, his mental image of the watchmaker will be correct.

This illustrates how God has revealed Himself to us. We are like the curious native and God's creative order is like the watch. *Creation and instinct tells us about God, but they can't help us know Him.* Creation and instinct tells us that God is "way out there somewhere beyond the vastness of the sky." We form mental images of what this God is like. But as with the native, most of them are wrong. God remains the unknown God.

The Apostle Paul met a group just like this in Greece. They were a very religious group because they had many altars. Paul noticed that one of the altars was dedicated "to the unknown God." They recognized the existence of God. But they did not know Him, so they worshiped Him in

12

ignorance. Paul took advantage of the opportunity and began to tell the group about "the unknown God." He said, "God, who made the world and everything in it, since He is Lord of heaven and earth, does not dwell in temples made with hands. Nor is He worshiped with men's hands, as though He needed anything, since He gives to all life, breath, and all things. And He has made from one blood every nation of men to dwell on all the face of the earth, and has determined their preappointed times and the boundaries of their habitation, so that they should seek the Lord, in the hope that they might grope for Him and find Him, though He is not far from each one of us; for in Him we live and move and have our being . . ." (Acts 17:24-28 NKJ).

God's Revelation in Writing

Since creation and instinct were not complete revelations, God determined to reveal Himself to us in a third way. He sent an instruction book to accompany the watch of His creative order and man's instinct. This instruction book is actually God's autobiography. We call it *the Bible*. It claims to be the inspired Word of God. (See 2 Timothy 3:16.) When we open the Bible we find that it says, "The world was made by God who takes great pride in His handiwork. And when He finished, He personally inspected it and pronounced it 'good.' To keep it in working order, read the following instructions." (See Genesis 1-2.)

Well, now we can begin to know the One Who made the world. We've got something in writing about Him. Now we can have correct understanding of Him. As we read God's Word, we find that He is different from His creatures. He's not at all what we've imagined Him to be.

His mighty acts of miracles tells us that He is all powerful. He says that He counts the stars and calls them by name to tell us that He is all-knowing. He tells us that He is everywhere present so that we can know there is no place we can go and be out of His sight. He says that He raises up kings and nations and puts them down to show us that He is sovereign. He demonstrates faithfulness to His Word to show us that He never changes.

He also tells us that He is love. He's not some distant deity who stands apart and aloof from our trials. Nor does He sit sternly in condemnation over us. On the contrary, He completely understands us and is able to fully and completely identify with all of our trials.

Since He made us, He understands our limitations. So He is sympathetic to our struggles. He remembers that we were born and shaped in iniquity. He knows that our brief journey on earth is but a fleeting moment in which we constantly war against the attacks of the world on our soul.

He knows our hearts because He knows our makeup. He was there before we were formed in our mother's womb. Therefore we can come to Him without pretense, just as we are. He will receive us with compassion, kindness, understanding and affection.

He is merciful and gracious towards us. He is slow to anger. He is good and ready to forgive. He has plenty of mercy. His lovingkindness is always extended to us.

He is righteous in all His ways and holy in all His works. Therefore, we can trust Him to always do the right thing by us.

Because He loves us, He must discipline us, but His discipline is always perfectly just. It is always fair and consistent for our own good. We can trust Him to move all events for the purpose of sharing His glory with us.

We are the constant object of His love and attention. His concern and care for us is never-ending. His patience, compassion, mercy, fairness and understanding are always extended to us. And even though He knows the worst about us, He still loves us. We can always expect a warm reception from Him.

Whatever our situation, we can have a calm assurance that He is ours and we are His. And as we get to know Him, His perfect love casts out all fear we may have of Him.

Is this the God you know? It can be. Because this is what God says about Himself in His autobiography. But even after reading it, man is still like the island native. He has learned a lot by reading the book, but he does not yet fully know God the way he should. He thinks that God is primarily concerned with outward acts. So man tries to approach God through religious ceremony and empty rituals. But God, through the Prophet Hosea, says, "For I desire mercy, not sacrifice, and acknowledgment of God rather than burnt offerings" (Hosea 6:6 NIV). You see, God was interested in man's heart, not his outward acts of religion.

God's Revelation in His Son

So, in order for man to fully know God, God decided that He would hold a town meeting. The town was planet earth. *God left His home in glory—the capitol of capitols—and came to planet earth to live among us so we could know Him.* He prepared a body for Himself in which to live. They called Him "Emmanuel" which means "God with us." He went by the name of Jesus of Nazareth. (See Matthew 1:23-25.)

The Apostle Paul describes what took place at this town meeting, which lasted for 33 years. In Philippians 2:6-11, he writes that Christ, "Who, being in very nature God, did not consider equality with God something to be grasped, but made himself nothing, taking the very nature of a servant, being made in human likeness. And being found in appearance as a man, he humbled himself and became obedient to death—even death on a cross! Therefore God exalted him to the highest place and gave him the name that is above every name, that at the name of Jesus every knee should bow, in heaven and on earth and under the earth, and every tongue confess that Jesus Christ is Lord, to the glory of God the Father" (NIV).

Toward the end of that town meeting, one of Jesus' disciples by the name of Philip said to Jesus, " 'Lord, show us the Father, and we shall be satisfied.' Jesus said to him, 'Have I been with you so long, and yet you do not know me, Philip? He who has seen me has seen the Father; how can you say, 'Show us the Father'? Do you not believe that I am

15

in the Father and the Father in me?' " (John 14:8-10 RSV). Drawing from our illustration of the island native, the watchmaker was here in the person of Jesus Christ.

Jesus Reveals God

John wrote about Jesus, "No one has seen God at any time. The only begotten Son, who is in the bosom of the Father, He has declared Him" (John 1:18 NKJ). Paul wrote in Colossians 1:15 that Jesus is the "image of the invisible God." The writer of Hebrews says that Jesus "bears the very stamp of God's nature" (Hebrews 1:3).

These phrases refer to the engraving on a coin. The engraving came from a stamp which was used to make the impression on the coin. Unless you work in the mint where the coin is made, you have never seen the stamp. But you can know exactly what it looks like, by looking at the coin.

Likewise, no one has ever seen God. But we can know exactly what He is like in His personal and moral being by looking at Jesus Christ. He is the picture of the creator that goes with His instruction book.

So God has revealed Himself to us in a fourth way, through His Son the Lord Jesus Christ. Colossians 2:9 says that "all the fullness of God" dwelled in Jesus Christ. He is the final and complete revelation of the unseen, unknown God.

How to Know God

Jesus said in Matthew 11:27, "All things have been delivered to me by my Father; and no one knows the Son except the Father, and no one knows the Father except the Son and anyone to whom the Son chooses to reveal him" (RSV). In this statement, Jesus says that He alone knows God. He further declares that no one can know God unless He (Jesus) makes God known to that person. But then He goes on to say that He desires to make God known to everyone. For His very next statement is, "Come to me, all who labor and are heavy laden, and I will give you rest. Take my yoke upon you, and learn from me; for I am gentle and lowly in heart, and you will find rest for your souls. For my yoke is easy, and my burden is light" (Matthew 11:28-30 RSV).

Jesus says that He will reveal God to anyone who will stop trying to find God in their own way and come to God through Him. In John 14:6, Jesus said, "I am the way, the truth, and the life. No one comes to the Father except through Me" (NKJ).

Again He said, "My sheep hear My voice, and I know them, and they follow Me. And I give them eternal life, and they shall never perish; neither shall anyone snatch them out of My hand. My Father, who has given them to Me, is greater than all; and no one is able to snatch them out of My Father's hand. I and My Father are one" (John 10:27-30 NKJ).

But then Jesus told His disciples that He would have to leave them. They didn't understand why He would leave them. He explained with these words, "If you love Me, keep My commandments. And I will pray the Father, and he will give you another Helper, that He may abide with you forever, even the Spirit of truth, whom the world cannot receive, because it neither sees Him nor knows Him; but you know Him, for He dwells with you and will be in you. I will not leave you orphans; I will come to you. A little while longer and the world will see Me no more, but you will see Me. Because I live, you will live also. At that day you will know that I am in My Father, and you in Me, and I in you. He who has My commandments and keeps them, it is he who loves Me. And he who loves Me will be loved by My Father, and I will love him and manifest Myself to him" (John 14:15-21 NKJ).

In these verses, Jesus was talking about sending the Holy Spirit to live in all who would receive Him. *In the Old Testament God was for us. In the New Testament He was with us. But now, God desires to be in us. By sending the Holy Spirit to live in us, Jesus would bring us into union with God so that we might know Him. This is how we come to know God. God will make Himself known to all who will come to Him through Jesus Christ. And you will know that you know Him because His Spirit, who will come to live in you, will reveal God to you with a personal intimacy which will bear witness to your heart that you have come to know God.* (See Romans 8:14-17.)

This was Jesus' great prayer for us in John 17:1-3 (NKJ), "Jesus spoke these words, lifted up His eyes to heaven, and said: 'Father, the hour has come. Glorify Your Son, that Your Son also may glorify You, as You have given Him authority over all flesh, that He should give eternal life to as many as You have given Him. And this is eternal life, that they may know You, the only true God, and Jesus Christ whom you have sent.' "

So yes, God wants us to know Him. He wants us to have intimate fellowship with Him. And this fellowship with God is available through the Lord Jesus Christ. When we ask Him to come into our life, He gives us the very Spirit of God. Jesus said it this way, "Behold, I stand at the door and knock. If anyone hears My voice and opens the door, I will come in to him and dine with him, and he with Me" (Revelation 3:20 NKJ).

Do you know God in the way I have described Him in this chapter? If not, please stop and pray right now, with a humble heart, for God to make Himself known to you. And then as you continue to read this book, it is my prayer that God will show Himself to you in a glorious way which perhaps you have never before known. May God bless you as we continue to look into the heart of God.

Chapter 2—Knowing God

Review Exercise 1

1. What does God mean when He says He wants us to know Him?

2. List the four ways in which God has made Himself known. Give a brief statement about each explaining how it is a revelation of God.

   a.

   b.

   c.

   d.

3. How can you apply this knowledge to your life?

3

God Is Self-Existing

One of the first things God tells us about Himself in the Bible is that He is *self-existing*. For God to be self-existing means that He has no origin. God was not created, nor did He proceed from, or evolve out of, anything. But in eternity past, God was alone. He was self-contained, self-sufficient, self-satisfied and in need of nothing. God was under no obligation to create anything. *But God chose to create as a sovereign act of His own will, determined by His own good pleasure and caused by nothing outside of Himself.* (See Revelation 4:11.)

The Self-Existing One

Now there are two revelations from God in the Bible that are particularly important in regard to His self-existence. The first is when God reveals His name to Moses. God had just commissioned Moses to lead the Hebrew people out of

Egypt. But Moses, knowing that the Hebrews would want to know who sent him, asks God His name. The following conversation between God and Moses is recorded in Exodus 3:13-14, "Then Moses said to God, 'Indeed, when I come to the children of Israel and say to them, "The God of your fathers has sent me to you," and they say to me, "What is His name?" what shall I say to them?' And God said to Moses 'I AM WHO I AM.' And He said, 'Thus you shall say to the children of Israel, "I AM has sent me to you" ' " (NKJ).

God reveals to Moses that His name is "I Am." Now this may not mean much to us, but it meant a great deal to Moses. For you see, in Bible times, a person's name was representative of the person himself. It indicated the person's nature and character. *"I Am" means self-existing, or uncaused.* So when God told Moses that His name was "I Am," He was saying to Moses that He was the self-existing, uncaused One. There was simply nothing adequate God could say about Himself to describe Himself except to say, "He was Himself."

In the New Testament, Jesus makes a statement that further clarifies the meaning of self-existence. He says, "For as the Father has life in Himself, so He has granted the Son to have life in Himself" (John 5:26 NKJ). In this statement, Jesus explains what self-existence means. He says it means to have life within one's self.

The Creator God has life within Himself. He has no origin, yet He Himself is the origin of all He creates. We live, and move and have our being in God (Acts 17:28). And this self-existing God creates life through His spoken Word. There is creative power in God's spoken Word. God speaks and life comes into existence. The writer of Hebrews put it in these words, "By faith we understand that the world was created by the word of God, so that what is seen was made out of things which do not appear" (Hebrews 11:3 RSV).

At a certain point in eternity past, God breathed life into man, and man became a living soul (Genesis 2:7). This life was to continuously flow in man unless man began to act as if he was the Creator. If that were to happen, this life would

22

stop flowing and man would experience something called death. (See Genesis 2:17.)

Now how does the creature act as if he is the Creator? The creature acts as if he is the Creator by denying God's claim on his life. He says, "I am independent. I have life within myself. I don't need God telling me what to do. I'm my own man. I'm doing my own thing. I'm self-sufficient. I am who I am."

So we see that the creature begins to act as if he is the Creator when he denies God's claim on his life. He acts as if he has life within himself. He seeks to live as if he is the self-existing one. He is sitting on the throne of his own life and worships himself as God.

When man denies God's sovereign claim over his life the result is death. And all human creatures have committed this sin. We have all denied God's claim on our life. The Bible calls this "independent spirit" sin. And the penalty for our sin is death (Romans 5:12).

But God so loved His human creatures that He gave His only Son, Who had life within Himself, to pay the sin penalty for us. And whoever will receive Him as their Lord and Savior will not perish but have everlasting life (John 3:16).

Eternal Life

How can God promise to give us eternal life? God can promise us eternal life because He has life within Himself. He imparts this life to us through Jesus Christ. God's life is eternal life so that all creatures who receive Jesus Christ receive eternal life through Christ giving us His Spirit, Who is eternal in Himself. Jesus spoke of this as being born again. Paul wrote these words to the Christians in Rome, "If the Spirit of him who raised Jesus from the dead dwells in you, he who raised Christ Jesus from the dead will give life to your mortal bodies also through his Spirit which dwells in you" (Romans 8:11 RSV).

Because God is self-existing, He is *eternal*. (See Psalms 90:2; 102:24; Habakkuk 1:12; 1 Timothy 1:17.) This means that God is *outside of time.* God deals with His creatures within a "time" framework. But time is a creature word that does not apply to God. Time only exists because we exist. Time did not begin with God, but it began when God created. God gives us the account of the beginning of time in Genesis 1:1 which says, "In the beginning God created."

But God Himself was before time. There never was a "time" when God did not exist, and there will never be a "time" when He ceases to exist. This is what the Bible means when it says that God is the "Alpha and Omega, the beginning and the end, the first and the last." (See Isaiah 41:4; 44:6; 48:12; Revelation 1:8, 11, 17; 21:6, 22:13.)

Creatures are always somewhere in relation to time. We're either past, present or future. George Washington lived in the past. We live in the now. Generations to come will live in the future. *But God, Who is eternal, always lives in the now.* Therefore, all of time, past, present and future is contained within God. He lived all of our yesterdays, and He's already lived all of our tomorrows. He is at the beginning and the end at the same "time." So God speaks of Himself as the One Who was and is and is to come (Revelation 1:8). All that God ever was, He is, and all that He is, He always will be.

Let me give you an example. God has blessed me with the privilege of writing several books. These books were in me. When I wrote the first words of the first page, I already knew what would be the last words on the last page. As the creator, or author in this example, I was in a different time frame than the characters in the book. In fact, I wasn't in a time frame at all. I was at the beginning and the end before the books were ever written. But the characters within the books appeared at a certain point in time (chapters) in the books. So even though I am outside the books, you can find me throughout their pages. They are my handiwork. And at any time while I was writing the books, I could whisper to the characters "I'm the beginning and the end."

Now since God is eternal, all that He is in Himself is eternal. His sovereign rule over His creation is eternal. His throne is established forever so that no usurper will ever

24

overthrow Him. Likewise, He is eternal in His all-knowledge, all-power, everywhere-presence and His unchangeableness. He is eternal in His holiness, love, justice and goodness. They are from everlasting to everlasting. This is a God worthy to be worshiped.

The Prophet Jeremiah said it in these words, "The steadfast love of the LORD never ceases, his mercies never come to an end; they are new every morning; great is thy faithfulness. 'The LORD is my portion,' says my soul, 'therefore I will hope in him' " (Lamentations 3:22-24 RSV). Jeremiah recognized that the eternal God was the only hope for fragile, finite creatures who live within time and must face death. Moses wrote, "The eternal God is your refuge . . ." (Deuteronomy 33:27 NKJ).

The eternal God has made eternal life available to us in Jesus Christ. This was Christ's claim when He said to Martha, " . . . 'I am the resurrection and the life. He who believes in Me, though he may die, he shall live. And whoever lives and believes in Me shall never die . . .' "(John 11:25-26 NKJ). Jesus also said in Revelation 1:18, "I am He who lives, and was dead, and behold, I am alive forevermore. Amen. And I have the keys of Hades and of Death" (NKJ).

The Apostle Peter wrote, "Blessed be the God and Father of our Lord Jesus Christ! By his great mercy we have been born anew to a living hope through the resurrection of Jesus Christ from the dead, and to an inheritance which is imperishable, undefiled, and unfading, kept in heaven for you, who by God's power are guarded through faith for a salvation ready to be revealed in the last time" (1 Peter 1:3-5 RSV). On this same thought, Paul wrote to the Christians in Colosse that Christ living in them was their hope of glory (Colossians 1:27).

Infinite Life

Because God is self-existing, He is also *infinite.* This means that God is *outside of space.* Therefore, He is limitless, boundless and measureless. Infinity is a term that

25

can only be applied to the creature. The creature is finite. He has limits and bounds and, therefore, he exists within space. The amount of space that my finite being occupies is about 5'10" high and 170 pounds. Now because I'm a finite creature with limits and bounds, the space I occupy can change. I can add to it by eating a lot of my wife's chocolate chip cookies, or I can take away from it by dieting. So you see, we creatures are always somewhere in relation to time and space.

But the self-existing, Creator God is different. He is outside of time and space. When King Solomon built the temple to God, he recognized this greatness of God and said, "But will God indeed dwell on the earth? Behold, heaven and the heaven of heavens cannot contain You. How much less this temple which I have built!" (1 Kings 8:27 NKJ). God said through the Prophet Jeremiah, " 'Can anyone hide himself in secret places, So I shall not see Him?' says the LORD: 'Do not I fill heaven and earth?' says the LORD" (Jeremiah 23:24 NKJ).

As time is contained within God, so is space. With God, there is no weight, distance or degrees. You cannot add to Him or take away from Him. *He is infinite in all that He is in Himself.* His sovereign rule is infinite. So is His all-knowledge, all-power, everywhere-presence and unchangeableness. He is infinite in His holiness, love, justice and goodness.

What Does it All Mean?

So, what does all of this mean to you personally? It means, for example, that there is nothing you can do to cause God to love you any more than He already does. Likewise, there is nothing you can do to cause God to love you any less than He already does. Love is not something God does, love is who God is in His being. Because He is infinite, you cannot add to, or take away from, His love. It is limitless, boundless and measureless. There is no sinner that God's mercy cannot forgive. For where sin abounds, God's grace does much more abound. God is Who He is in Himself and everything

26

that flows out of Him is infinite.

God's self-existence means, then, that He is above and outside of time and space. Therefore, He is above and outside of everything that is within time and space like us creatures. But, at the same time, God tells us that He wants us to know Him. *The question of all ages is, "How can we know a God Who is above us and outside of us?"* God tells us the answer through the Prophet Isaiah, "For thus says the High and lofty One Who inhabits eternity, whose name is Holy: 'I dwell in the high and holy place, With him who has a contrite and humble spirit, To revive the spirit of the humble, And to revive the heart of the contrite ones' " (Isaiah 57:15 NKJ). (See also Isaiah 60:1-2.)

God is far away in His greatness, but at the same time He draws near to those who humble themselves before Him. James wrote " '. . . God resists the proud, But gives grace to the humble.' Therefore submit to God. Resist the devil and he will flee from you. Draw near to God and He will draw near to you. Cleanse your hands, you sinners; and purify your hearts, you double-minded. Lament and mourn and weep! Let your laughter be turned to mourning and your joy to gloom. Humble yourselves in the sight of the Lord, and He will lift you up" (James 4:6-10 NKJ).

God lifts up through His Son Jesus Christ, Who was infinity in the flesh. This is what the writer of Hebrews meant when he said that Jesus Christ is the same yesterday, today and forever (Hebrew 13:8). God has entered into time and space through the person of the Lord Jesus Christ so that we might draw near to Him and know Him.

You can know Him right now by humbling yourself before Him. You do this by confessing to God that you, at times, have lived as though you were your own God. But now you realize that this is sin. And you want to turn from this attitude of pride and self-sufficiency and bow your knee before the eternal, infinite God Who came to earth in the person of Jesus Christ.

Review Exercise 2

1. Give a brief definition of the word "self-existing."

2. God's self-existence includes two primary aspects about His being. Name these two aspects and give a brief explanation as to how they apply to God.

    a.

    b.

3. How can you apply this knowledge to your life?

4

God Is a Personal Spirit

In this chapter we are going to learn two further revelations which God gives about Himself in the pages of the Bible. These two are that God is *spirit* and God is *personal.* We'll begin with the first and then consider the personal nature of God.

God Is Spirit

On one occasion, Jesus was walking from Judea to Galilee and passed through the area of Samaria. As the journey was long and hot, Jesus grew tired and stopped at Jacob's well for water. While He was there, a Samaritan woman came to the well to draw water. Jesus told the woman that He could give her living water that would quench her spiritual thirst.

Then Jesus revealed to the woman certain things about her past that He would not have known unless God had made them known to Him. This prompted the following conversation between Him and the woman: "The woman said to Him, 'Sir, I perceive that you are a prophet. Our fathers worshiped on this mountain, and you Jews say that in Jerusalem is the place where one ought to worship.' Jesus said to her, 'Woman, believe me, the hour is coming when you will neither on this mountain, nor in Jerusalem, worship the Father. You worship what you do not know; we know what we worship, for salvation is of the Jews. But the hour is coming, and now is, when the true worshipers will worship the Father in spirit and truth; for the Father is seeking such to worship Him. God is Spirit, and those who worship Him must worship Him in spirit and truth' " (John 4:19-24 NKJ).

In the year 721 B.C. the Assyrians conquered the area known as Samaria. The King of Assyria imported foreigners into the land who intermarried with the remnant left there. The result was a people who were part Jew and part Gentile. This mixed race of people were called Samaritans. During the time of Nehemiah, a Samaritan named Sanballat built a temple on Mount Gerizim, which was north of Jerusalem. This was where the Samaritans worshiped and this is the place to which the woman is referring. We would think of it as their church building. The Jews, on the other hand, worshiped God at the temple in Jerusalem. This was their church building.

Now something had puzzled this woman for many years, she wanted to know which was the right church house. Which is the true place of worship? Where is God to be found? Which denomination, Gerizimites or Jerusalemites, should she join? Which church should she attend? Believing Jesus to be a prophet, she thought perhaps He could tell her.

Many people ask this same question today. They are confused by the many different religious denominations and organizations which all claim to be the real place to find God. So it is important to look closely at Jesus' answer.

Today, many people would answer the woman by telling her that she must join their particular religious organization. But Jesus answered differently. *Jesus told the woman that the day was coming when a person would not have to "go*

30

somewhere" to worship God. But they would be able to worship God out of their own spirit in communion with the Holy Spirit, whom Jesus would send. The Holy Spirit would take us right into the presence of God regardless of where we might be physically. In other words, we wouldn't "go to church," but we ourselves would be the church through our receiving the Holy Spirit.

This completely baffles those who are religious and profess Christianity but who do not possess Christ. They just cannot understand how anybody can worship God unless they are at a church building on Sunday morning from 11:00-12:00 going through some religious form and ritual. Paul explains the reason why they cannot understand in 1 Corinthians 2:14, "But the natural man does not receive the things of the Spirit of God, for they are foolishness to him; nor can he know them, because they are spiritually discerned" (NKJ).

Because God is spirit, true worship flows out of a human spirit that has been renewed by the Holy Spirit. Therefore, religious form and ritual is not true worship unless the worshipers themselves have been made alive through a spiritual rebirth. As Jesus told the religious leader named Nicodemus, "you must be born again" (see John 3:1-7).

Now since God is a spirit who is everywhere present, you can worship Him anytime and at any place. King Solomon realized this when he built the temple in Jerusalem. He said in 1 Kings 8:27, "But will God indeed dwell on the earth? Behold, heaven and the heaven of heavens cannot contain you. How much less this temple that I have built!" (NKJ). Luke writes on this same thought, "God, who made the world and everything in it, since He is Lord of heaven and earth, does not dwell in temples made with hands" (Acts 17:24 NKJ).

Now if God does not dwell in temples made with hands, where does He dwell? He dwells in the hearts of all who have received Him. Paul said it this way, "Or do you not know that your body is the temple of the Holy Spirit who is in you, whom you have from God, and you are not your own?"

31

(1 Corinthians 6:19 NKJ).

Worship is based on a person, not a place. It's centered on "who," not "where." Worship is exalting Jesus Christ as Lord through the testimony of the Holy Spirit to your heart. Much that goes under the name of worship is not really worship at all. It is merely a satisfying of man's religious obligations and a soothing of his seared conscience. If you must have religious form and ritual to feel close to God, you are not at all close to Him. You have missed the whole point of worship. You are trying to approach God through your physical senses rather than through a spirit that has been made alive through faith in Jesus Christ.

Since God exists in the spiritual realm, He cannot be apprehended by the physical senses. Paul wrote in 1 Corinthians 2:9-10, " '. . . Eye has not seen, nor ear heard, Nor have entered into the heart of man The things which God has prepared for those who love Him.' But God has revealed them to us by His Spirit. For the Spirit searches all things, yes, the deep things of God" (NKJ).

God, as a spirit, does not have a physical body. After Jesus was resurrected, He appeared to His followers and said, "Behold My hands and My feet, that it is I Myself. Handle Me and see, for a spirit does not have flesh and bones as you see I have" (Luke 24:39 NKJ).

Yet, God is described in the Bible as having ears, eyes, feet, hands, arms, etc. The Bible says that God feels, sees, hears, walks and talks. These are expressions of God's being put in human terms so that we can understand Him. They are not meant to be literal, in the sense, for example, that God has a physical body. The only way the infinite God can be understood by finite creatures is by God speaking of Himself in terms we can understand. For example, when we speak of God's arm we are referring to His all-power. When we speak of His eyes we are referring to His all-knowledge. When we speak of God's heart we are referring to His perfect love, and so forth.

Because God is a spirit without a physical body, we cannot see Him. John 1:18 says that no one has seen God at any time. We read in Colossians 1:15 and 1 Timothy 1:17 that God is invisible. However, the invisible, unseen God has, on occasion, chosen to manifest Himself in visible form to communicate with His creatures. For example, He appeared as a man to visit with Abraham (Genesis 18:2-3). Moses saw His back (Genesis 33:23). Jacob wrestled with Him (Genesis 32:30, 33:10). But these were only manifestations of God in visible form.

Since no one has seen God as He is, there is nothing we can make to represent Him. There is no image we can make with our hands or picture in our mind that can truthfully portray Him. So, God forbids us to try to make such an image. (See Exodus 20:4-6; Deuteronomy 4:15-24; Isaiah 40:18-25.) Regardless of how sincere we may be, any image we make of God is a misrepresentation of Him. *History has proven that whenever we have made images of God, we always worship that image as a true representation of God, which it is not.* The problem is that we begin to think that God is like the image we have made. And since we associate God with the image, we begin to get all kinds of false ideas of what God is like.

Let me give you a couple of examples. If we put Jesus on the cross and look at that symbol as a reminder that Jesus died for our sins, we've made an idol. Now, here is the reason. Jesus is not on the cross. He is in heaven, the cross is bare, the tomb is empty—Jesus lives! We are representing God as the suffering Savior. This is true as far as it goes. But Jesus is much more than a suffering Savior. He is also our great high priest who ever lives to make intercession for us. Jesus on the cross cannot represent this aspect of Christ's ministry. So Jesus on the cross as a symbol is an untruthful representation of God. If this is your image of Christ, then you will, by necessity, look to someone else to be your mediator, such as Mary. The result is that Mary is exalted as your mediator while Jesus is still dead on the cross.

Another example is the golden calf that the Hebrews made when they came out of Egypt. (See Exodus 32.) That calf represented power. The Hebrews worshiped the calf and said that it was the calf that brought them out of Egypt. But Aaron said, as they worshiped the calf, that it was a feast to the "Lord" (Exodus 32:5). They were worshiping the calf as a representation of God. But the calf only represented God's power, so it was an idol. If we worship God only for His power and follow after signs and wonders without allowing Him to work holiness in our life, we've made ourselves a golden calf. God is more than just power. God is all that He is and no image can represent Him.

So you see, an idol is not just something unbelievers worship. Christians may also find themselves worshiping idols. Do you have a golden calf? God is spirit.

God Is Personal

God is also personal. *What do we mean when we say God is personal? We mean that the Creator God possesses a personality that includes self-consciousness and self-determination.* Self-consciousness is the ability to know who you are. It is an awareness of self. As a human, you have a personality. You have feelings. You have certain traits and characteristics. You are very much aware of your behavior, appearance, etc. You have a sense of your being, and attitudes about yourself. This is what it means to be self-conscious. Self-determination means that you have the ability to bring about a course of action out of your own free will. So if you don't like yourself because you are over-weight, you can lose weight and perhaps have a better self-image.

Human personality is one of the differences between people and animals. For example, I have a dog. My dog can stare at himself in the mirror and not know that he is staring at himself. This is because my dog is not aware of himself. He has consciousness but not self-consciousness. And when his food bowls are empty, he knocks them all over the house so my wife and I will know he needs more food. But he cannot get the food out of the bag and put it in his bowl for himself. He has determination but not self-determination. He cannot bring about a course of action out of his own free will.

As a personal Creator, God knows Himself. He gave the greatest declaration of self-consciousness the world has ever known when he said, "I Am That I Am." (See Exodus 3:14.) That means God is never going to do anything to surprise Himself, for which He is later sorry. God knows that He is good, so everything He does will be good. God knows that He is holy, so everything He does will be holy. God knows that He is just, so everything He does will be just. God knows that He is love, so everything He does will be done out of love.

We don't completely know our hearts (Jeremiah 17:9-10), so we often say and do things that surprise ourselves. Not so with God. *God perfectly knows Himself.* He is the ultimate self-conscious person. And God has all power to bring about whatever course of action He wills. He is a personal God and has made us personal beings that we might know Him.

It is absolutely essential that we have this understanding of God. *This is because your concept and understanding of God affects everything in your life.* It is the ruling force that dictates how you live. The study of "God Himself" is the most important study to which you can ever give yourself. If you neglect this study, you will be like the native we talked about in a previous chapter. You will develop false concepts and ideas about God which will destroy you.

False Concepts of God

I want to briefly comment on two false concepts of God. These are *pantheism* and *deism.* Pantheism is the philosophy and concept of God of all Eastern religions including those that have made their way to the United States. Pantheism teaches that God is in everything and everything is in God. God is considered to be one with all He has created rather than, as the Bible teaches, separate from creation. God is considered to be an impersonal principle, influence or spirit force that exists in nature and is one with nature. God is said to be, for example, in the stars, in the trees, in the grass, in the animals, in the dirt, in man. This is a perversion of the biblical teaching that God is everywhere present. It reduces man, who was made in the image of God, to the level of dirt. But as we have already learned, God is outside of and separate from His creation.

Now let me show you how this false concept of God affects human lives. I'm told that in a reasonably good year, the country of India can grow enough grain to feed its entire population of 620 million people and still have grain left over to export. But every year, one-third to one-half of the grain crop is eaten by rats. Yet the people will not kill the rats because of their pantheistic concept of God. So the children starve to death and the country remains in poverty, starvation and ignorance.

Deism teaches that there is a personal God who created the universe but is not personally active in its affairs. Since God is not considered personally active in the universe, then there is no value in prayer. If there is no value in prayer, then there's no hope in this life. Man is left to his own destiny and eventually becomes fatalistic. In other words, you cannot really know God.

So you see, your concept of God does determine how you live. God is personal. He created man as a personal being with whom He desires to share His glory. God says His relationship to us is like a father to his son, a shepherd to his sheep, a groom to his bride and a king to his servants. He is active in the world He created moving the course of world events for the good to those who love Him and are called to share His glory. *The Creator of the universe is a personal God who has revealed Himself to us in time and space in the person of the Lord Jesus Christ so that we might know Him and worship Him out of a spirit that has been made alive by grace through faith.*

Do you know Him yet? If not, ask Him to reveal Himself to you in a personal way through a revelation of the person of Jesus Christ. And, if you already know Him, I pray that you will seek the pure spiritual worship that is pleasing to Him, for it is to these worshipers that God reveals Himself.

Chapter 4—God Is a Personal Spirit

Review Exercise 3

1. What does it mean to worship God in spirit and truth?

2. What do we mean when we say that God is personal?

3. Define the following terms:

    a. Pantheism-

    b. Deism-

4. How can you apply this knowledge to your life?

5

God Is Three in One

Perhaps the most difficult to understand revelation which God gives us about Himself is that there is only one God who yet exists in three persons. This is the biblical teaching known as the *"Trinity of God."* As with many Christian terms, the actual word "trinity" is not found in the Bible. It is simply a term which man has used to describe this revelation of God's nature.

The fact that God exists in a trinity is taught in the very first chapter of the Bible and is progressively revealed throughout the Old Testament. When we come to the New Testament, we learn that the relationship of this trinity is Father, Son, and Holy Spirit.

Christians do not worship three gods. Neither do we worship one God who has manifested Himself in three ways or offices. But we worship one God who has revealed Himself to exist in three distinct coequal personalities.

These divine personalities are of the same nature, or essence, which means that they have the same attributes and are equally worthy of worship and praise. Yet, each has a different role in the redemption, or salvation, of man.

The Meaning of One

Before we look into this aspect of God's nature, we must first understand the biblical use of the word "one." When the Hebrews came out of Egypt, the whole world worshiped idols. God chose to use the Hebrew people to show the world that He alone was God. So He spoke to them through Moses and said, "Hear, O Israel: The LORD our God, the LORD is one!" (Deuteronomy 6:4 NKJ). This statement became the great Jewish declaration of faith in the one true God. And throughout the Old Testament, God reminded the Hebrews that He alone was the one true God and there was no God beside Him. (See Isaiah 44:6-8, 45:5; 1 Timothy 2:5; 1 Corinthians 8:4.)

Now when we read that God says He is the one true God, we automatically think that He is talking in the absolute sense of the word, like the number one. For example, if I say to my wife, "you are my one true love," I mean that in the absolute sense of the word. She is the only one. The Hebrews had a word they could have used to speak of God's oneness in this absolute sense, but they did not use this word. They used a different Hebrew word. The Hebrew word they used speaks of God's oneness in a collective sense rather than an absolute sense.

For example, the Bible speaks of the husband and wife becoming one flesh (Genesis 2:24). This refers to their physical unity, but they are still two different people. When Nimrod built the Tower of Babel, the whole world began to come under his influence. God said, ". . . Indeed the people are one . . ." (Genesis 11:6 NKJ). Now there were many people, but they had a collective unity around Nimrod. In the Book of Acts, the early Christians came together as one. (See Acts 2:1, 4:24, 32.) In John 17:22, Jesus prayed that His followers would be one. This was a prayer for unity.

40

So the meaning of the word "one" in reference to God speaks of His unity. There is only one God absolutely speaking, but He exists in three persons having perfect unity between themselves. It is important to have this biblical understanding of the word "one." It will clear up many Scriptures that may have puzzled you in the past. Let's now look through the Old Testament at some of the more obvious references to God as a trinity then we will see its full revelation in the New Testament.

Trinity in the Old Testament

Genesis 1:1 says, "In the beginning God created the heaven and the earth" (NKJ). The Hebrew word for God in this verse is Elohim. Elohim is the plural form of the singular word "El," which means God. El means God; Elohim means Gods. So Genesis 1:1 actually says, "In the beginning Gods created the heaven and the earth." However, in the Bible, the plural noun Elohim is used gramatically with a singular verb. Now we don't have to be experts in the English language to know that we don't use plural nouns with singular verbs. We do not say, "Gods is on the throne" unless there is one God who exists in more than one person. So in the very first verse in the Bible, God is telling us something very special about Himself. And He makes this "something special" very clear to us throughout the rest of the Bible.

In Genesis 1:26, God says, ". . . Let Us make man in Our image according to Our likeness . . ." (NKJ). Who is this "us" and "our" about whom God is speaking? Some people would say it is angels. But it can't be angels because the next verse says that God created man in His own image. So here God begins to speak of Himself using plural pronouns.

God next speaks about Himself in this way when He was forced to banish Adam and Eve from the garden. Genesis 3:22 says, "Then the LORD God said, 'Behold, the man has become like one of Us . . .' " (NKJ). Note the plural pronoun "us" in reference to God.

When Nimrod built the Tower of Babel, God determined that He would confuse the people's language and scatter

41

them all over the earth. He spoke of Himself as a plural personality by saying, "Come, let Us go down and there confuse their language, that they may not understand one another's speech" (Genesis 11:7 NKJ).

Then later, Isaiah heard God talking to Himself about the need for a prophet in the land. And God said, ". . . who will go for us?" (Isaiah 6:8 NKJ).

These and many other places in the Bible reveal to us that God has a perfect unity with Himself while at the same time speaks of Himself as if more than one person is involved.

The Angel of the Lord

Then God began to give us more insight into His triune nature through an unusual Old Testament character called *"the angel of the Lord."* You will find Him throughout the Old Testament, but in this discussion, we will just note a few of His appearances.

The angel of the Lord is first mentioned in the Bible in His appearance to Hagar, Sarah's Egyptian handmaid. The angel of the Lord promises to multiply Hagar's seed. No ordinary angel could make that kind of promise. Hagar responds by calling this angel, "Lord." (See Genesis 16:7-13.)

We next see the angel of the Lord with Abraham. God had told Abraham to offer Isaac as a sacrifice to prove his devotion to God. But just before Isaac was harmed, God interceded. Genesis 22:11-12 says, "But the Angel of the LORD called to him from heaven and said, 'Abraham, Abraham!' And he said, 'Here I am.' And He said, 'Do not lay your hand on the lad, or do anything to him; for now I know that you fear God, seeing you have not withheld your son, your only son, from Me' " (NKJ). The angel of the Lord speaks of Himself as God. Then, in verses 16 to 17 He swears by Himself as Lord and promises to multiply Abraham's seed.

We next find the angel of the Lord appearing to Moses. It was a most dramatic appearance that Moses would never forget. He records the encounter for us in Exodus 3:2-4,

"And the angel of the LORD appeared to him in a flame of fire out of the midst of a bush; and he looked, and lo, the bush was burning, yet it was not consumed. And Moses said, 'I will turn aside and see this great sight, why the bush is not burnt.' When the LORD saw that he turned aside to see, God called to him out of the bush, 'Moses, Moses!' And he said, 'Here am I' " (RSV). These verses say that the angel of the Lord appeared to Moses in the burning bush but that it was actually God who spoke out of the midst of the bush.

And it was God, in the angel of the Lord, who led the Hebrews to their promised land. Exodus 13:21 says, "And the LORD went before them by day in a pillar of cloud to lead the way, and by night in a pillar of fire to give them light, so as to go by day and night" (NKJ). Yet later, we are told that it was the angel of the Lord who went before them, "And the Angel of God, who went before the camp of Israel, moved and went behind them; and the pillar of cloud went before them and stood behind them" (Exodus 14:19 NKJ).

In this same setting, God makes an extraordinary claim about the angel of the Lord. He says, "Behold, I send an Angel before you to keep you in the way and to bring you into the place which I have prepared. Beware of Him and obey His voice; do not provoke Him, for He will not pardon your transgressions; for My name is in Him. But if you indeed obey His voice and do all that I speak, then I will be an enemy to your enemies and an adversary to your adversaries. For My angel will go before you . . ." (Exodus 23:20-23 NKJ).

In these examples, we see a person called the angel of the Lord, yet it is clear that He is more than just an ordinary angel. He is God, yet in some way, distinct from God. And although the Hebrew people didn't quite understand it themselves, they recognized the angel of the Lord as God Himself communicating to them in a special way. And it is very interesting to note that, after Jesus is born, the angel of the Lord is no longer mentioned in the Bible. He just disappears from view.

It seems that the angel of the Lord was actually a

manifestation of Christ in the Old Testament. As the eternal Son of God and part of the Trinity of God, Christ was doing on a temporal basis, through the angel of the Lord, what He would one day do permanently when He prepared for Himself a body and came to the earth in the person of Jesus of Nazareth.

The Spirit of God

The Spirit of God is also seen throughout the Old Testament. Let's now consider some of His activities. The second verse in the Bible says, ". . . And the Spirit of God was hovering over the face of the waters" (Genesis 1:2 NKJ). Here we see the Spirit of God active in creation.

It was the Spirit of God who gave Joseph the interpretation to Pharaoh's dream. Pharaoh recognized this and said to his servants, "Can we find such a man as this, in whom is the Spirit of God?" (Genesis 41:38 RSV).

When God gave instructions to the Hebrews to build a tabernacle, He equipped a certain builder for the task by filling him with His Spirit. In Exodus 31:1-3, we read, "Then the LORD spoke to Moses, saying: 'See, I have called by name Bezaleel the son of Uri, the son of Hur, of the tribe of Judah. And I have filled him with the Spirit of God, in wisdom, in understanding, in knowledge, and in all manner of workmanship' " (NKJ).

God chose Joshua to lead the people to their promised land, and it was the Spirit of God in Joshua who enabled Joshua to perform the task. Numbers 27:18 reads, "And the LORD said to Moses: 'Take Joshua the son of Nun with you, a man in whom is the Spirit, and lay your hand on him' " (NKJ). There may be more to this passage than meets the eye. Joshua's Hebrew name (Yeshua) is the same name for Jesus. Joshua's father's name is Nun. Nun means everlasting. So here is an Old Testament character whose Hebrew name is the same as Jesus, and his commission is to lead the people into their land. He has the Spirit of God in him and his father's name means everlasting. Could it be that God was using these names and relationships to teach us about His triune nature?

In Isaiah 63:7-11, there is a reference to the Lord, the angel of the Lord and to God's Spirit who is called the Holy Spirit. *Throughout the Old Testament there is a progressive unfolding revelation of the Trinity of God.* But it's not until we come to the New Testament that we understand this relationship as Father, Son and Holy Spirit.

God's Spoken Word
We can better understand the way the New Testament presents the Trinity of God if we know the Jewish viewpoint of the spoken word. When a person spoke a word, the Hebrew considered that word which came out of the person's mouth as a living thing in itself. The word was one with the person because it came out of that person and represented that person's self. But once it was spoken, it was not only one with the person, but it became a living thing in itself having the nature of the one who spoke. The word was one with the person, yet once it was spoken, it became distinct from the person. This spoken word, as a living thing in itself, would actually go and accomplish that which had been spoken.

When the Old Testament says that "The word of the Lord" came to someone, the Hebrews believed that it was God Himself coming to accomplish that which He had spoken. Several places in the Old Testament makes this very clear. Isaiah 55:11 reads, "So shall My word be that goes forth from My mouth; It shall not return to Me void, But it shall accomplish what I please, And it shall prosper in the thing for which I sent it" (NKJ). Here we see that God's word is considered to be one with God Himself, yet a distinct person from Him, going to accomplish that which He has spoken.

Another clear example is Isaiah 45:22-23 where God says, "Look to Me, and be saved, All you ends of the earth! For I am God, and there is no other. I have sworn by Myself; The word has gone out of My mouth in righteousness, And shall not return, That to Me every knee shall bow, Every tongue shall take an oath" (NKJ). Here again we see that God is sending out His word to accomplish something. And what does this passage say the word is going to accomplish? It says that God's word will cause every knee to bow before God and every tongue confess that He is Lord. The word who is one with God, yet distinct from God, will accomplish this.

The same idea was associated with the breath, or Spirit, of God. It was one with God, yet when it went out from God, it became a separate and distinct person who would go and accomplish God's will.

Trinity in the New Testament

With this Old Testament background, we can better understand the Trinity of God as it is more fully revealed in the New Testament. John began his Gospel from this point of view. He said, "In the beginning was the Word, and the Word was with God, and the Word was God. He was in the beginning with God. All things were made through Him, and without Him nothing was made that was made. In Him was life, and the life was the light of men" (John 1:1-4 NKJ).

We can now understand what John is talking about and how he can say that the Word was God while at the same time with God. *The Word was God because it was part of God, one with God, and having the same nature as God.* Yet at the same time, the Word was with God as a separate, distinct living personality. And the Word, who was God, would go out from God to accomplish something. So John wrote, "And the Word became flesh and dwelt among us, and we beheld His glory, the glory as of the only begotten of the Father, full of grace and truth" (John 1:14 NKJ).

John does not say that the Word was made, but that the Word was made flesh. *The Word, who was God, came out of God and prepared for Himself a physical body in order to accomplish something. God became a man in the person of Jesus of Nazareth.* The writer of Hebrews puts it this way, "God, who at various times and in different ways spoke in time past to the fathers by the prophets, has in these last days spoken to us by His Son, whom He has appointed heir of all things, through whom also He made the worlds" (Hebrews 1:1-2 NKJ).

46

Jesus upheld the Old Testament revelation concerning the oneness, or unity, of God. When one of the religious leaders asked Jesus which was the greatest commandment, Jesus replied ". . . 'Hear, O Israel, the LORD our God, the LORD is one' " (Mark 12:29 NKJ). Now we know what Jesus meant because we understand the meaning of the word one. Jesus was talking about the unity of God. *There is only one God, but He exists in three persons having perfect unity between themselves.*

This is most clearly seen in Jesus' prayer which is recorded in John 17. You would benefit by reading that entire chapter, looking for key words and phrases which present Christ Jesus as the Word of God, who was one with God, yet came out of God to planet earth in order to accomplish a particular work.

Now what did God come to accomplish through Jesus Christ? Paul tells us in Philippians 2:5-11, "Your attitude should be the same as that of Christ Jesus: Who, being in the very nature God, did not consider equality with God something to be grasped, but made himself nothing, taking the very nature of a servant, being made in human likeness. And being found in appearance as a man, he humbled himself and became obedient to death—even death on a cross! Therefore God exalted him to the highest place and gave him the name that is above every name, that at the name of Jesus every knee should bow, in heaven and on earth and under the earth, and every tongue confess that Jesus is Lord, to the glory of God the Father" (NIV).

Now this is what we just read in Isaiah 45:23. The Isaiah passage said that every tongue would confess that God is Lord, while the Philippians statement says that every tongue will confess that Jesus is Lord. They are one, yet distinct persons. The Hebrews believed that God would, in some way, come and redeem them as their Messiah. Christ, which means Messiah, was God coming to redeem the world through Jesus, the Word who became flesh. Even when Jesus returns to planet earth to establish His kingdom, He is called the *Word of God* (Revelation 19:13).

47

Many people say that Jesus never claimed to be God. This is simply not true. Why, even at His birth, they referred to Him as Emmanuel, which means "God with us" (Matthew 1:18-25). *Jesus claimed to be God by His words and His works, and the Jews knew very well this was His claim.* They just didn't believe (John 10:24-38, 14:7-11).

When Satan tempted Jesus to worship him, Jesus responded by saying, "Begone, Satan! for it is written, 'You shall worship the Lord your God and him only shall you serve' " (Matthew 4:10 RSV). Yet, Jesus Himself accepted worship (Matthew 9:18, 14:33, 15:25, 20:20, 28:17; Luke 24:52; John 9:38).

Jesus claimed to be one with God (John 14:7-11, 10:24-38, 17:21-23). He is called God many times in the New Testament. (See John 5:18, 10:33, 20:28; Philippians 2:5-11; Colossians 1:15-19; Titus 2:13; 1 John 5:20.)

People are often confused about the deity of Jesus Christ because the Bible also calls Him the Son of God. This confusion comes about because of a misunderstanding of the meaning of the phrase "Son of." *The phrase "Son of" means "one with the same nature as, or of the same likeness."* Therefore, Son of God means one with the same nature as God or of the same likeness as God. This can only be God Himself. *So every time Jesus spoke of Himself as the Son of God, He was claiming to be God.* You and I may have been confused about this, but the Jews weren't. They knew exactly what He meant. (See John 5:18, 10:33-36.) Son of God literally means, "God the Son."

Jesus also referred to Himself as the Son of man. This just means that He was like man in that He was a real human person. Here is how the writer of Hebrews says it, "Since the children have flesh and blood, he too shared in their humanity so that by his death he might destroy him who holds the power of death—that is, the devil—and free those who all their lives were held in slavery by their fear of death" (Hebrews 2:14-15 NIV). Son of man in relation to Jesus means, "God the man."

Christ (Messiah) is the divine part of the name of God in

the flesh and corresponds to the phrase "Son of God." Jesus is the human part of the name of God in the flesh and corresponds to the phrase "Son of man." Therefore, Christ is the God-man.

In John 14:23, Jesus said that He and the Father would come and live in anyone who would receive His words. *Now how are they going to do that?* They do that through the person of God the Holy Spirit. We mentioned earlier that in the Old Testament, God was said to be for His people. In the New Testament God was with His people. But with the giving of the Spirit, God is now in His people.

Jesus said to His disciples, "And I will pray the Father, and He will give you another Helper, that He may abide with you forever, even the Spirit of truth, whom the world cannot receive, because it neither sees Him nor knows Him; but you know Him, for He dwells with you and will be in you" (John 14:16-17 NKJ). (See also John 15:26; 16:6, 13.)

Before Jesus left His disciples, He promised to send them another Helper who would be in them. Who is the first Helper? The first Helper is obviously Jesus Himself. Jesus was with them. But as a flesh and blood person Himself, Jesus could not get inside of them. So He promised to send another Helper who would come to live in them. The other Helper is the Holy Spirit who comes to live in all who will receive Jesus as their Lord and Savior. The Greek word for helper means "another just like the first one."

Jesus speaks of the Holy Spirit as a divine person like Himself who will come and live in them, giving them eternal life and helping them to know and walk with God. So the Holy Spirit is not an "it" or an "impersonal influence," but He is a divine person who is part of the Trinity of God equal in all ways to both the Father and the Son. The Bible refers to the Holy Spirit using personal pronouns, credits Him with works that can only be performed by an actual person and says that He relates and interacts with humans in a personal manner.

After Jesus was resurrected, He appeared to His disciples and gave the Holy Spirit to them. John records it for us,

"Then Jesus said to them again, 'Peace be with you. As my Father has sent Me, I also send you.' And when He had said this, He breathed on them, and said to them, 'Receive the Holy Spirit' " (John 20:21-22 NKJ). *The breath of life who was one with God, but a distinct person in Himself, was God's very own Spirit going out of God to accomplish that which God had spoken.*

A number of New Testament statements speak of the Trinity of God directly. One is when Jesus was baptized. Matthew writes, "Then Jesus, when He had been baptized, came up immediately from the water; and behold, the heavens were opened to Him, and He saw the Spirit of God descending like a dove and alighting upon Him. And suddenly a voice came from heaven saying, 'This is My beloved Son, in whom I am well pleased' " (Matthew 3:16-17 NKJ).

Jesus refers to the Trinity of God in the following commission He gave to His disciples, "Go therefore and make disciples of all the nations, baptizing them in the name of the Father and of the Son and of the Holy Spirit" (Matthew 28:19 NKJ).

Paul acknowledged the Trinity of God in closing out his letter to the Corinthians, "The grace of our Lord Jesus Christ and the love of God, and the communion of the Holy Spirit be with you all. Amen" (2 Corinthians 13:14 NKJ).

Trinity of God in Redemption

So we see, there is one God who exists in three persons known as the Father, the Son and the Holy Spirit. We collectively refer to these three as the Godhead. Although they are one, each has a *different role* in the redemption or salvation of man.

Man is also a trinity consisting of body, soul and spirit (1 Thessalonians 5:23). Each member of the Godhead, Father, Son and Holy Spirit, redeems a different part of man. God the Son, Jesus Christ, redeems man's spirit from the penalty of sin. The Bible uses the word *justification* to refer to this aspect of redemption (Romans 3:20-25, 5:1, Galatians 2:16).

This is a past act by God the Son in the life of every Christian.

Presently, God the Holy Spirit, is redeeming the Christian's soul from the power of sin. The Bible refers to this act of redemption as *sanctification* (2 Thessalonians 2:13; 1 Peter 1:2).

In the future, God the Father will redeem our bodies even from the presence of sin. The Bible uses the word *glorification* to speak of this work of redemption (Romans 8:28-30; 2 Timothy 2:10; 1 Peter. 5:10).

So the Christian has been saved (justified), is being saved (sanctified) and will be saved (glorified) by the redeeming grace of the triune God (Ephesians 2:8-10).

Have you been redeemed? Jesus Christ died to save your spirit from the penalty of sin. This penalty is death, which is eternal separation from God. But Jesus came that you might have life and have it more abundantly (John 10:10). If you have been justified, will you allow the Holy Spirit to rule over your soul and give you victory over the power of sin? And may you walk in hope knowing that ". . . it does not yet appear what we shall be, but we know that when he appears we shall be like him, for we shall see him as he is" (1 John 3:2 RSV).

Chapter 5—God Is Three in One

Review Exercise 4

1. Define the biblical meaning of the word "one" as it is used in Deuteronomy 6:4.

2. Briefly explain how the Trinity of God is revealed in the Old Testament.

3. Briefly explain how the Trinity of God is revealed in the New Testament.

4. How does the Trinity of God work as a unit to redeem man?

5. How can you apply this knowledge to your life?

PART 2
GOD'S MAJESTIC ATTRIBUTES

6
God Is Sovereign

In this chapter we are going to examine the biblical revelation that God is sovereign. Psalms 47:6-8 reads, "Sing praises to God, sing praises! For God is the king of all the earth; sing praises with a psalm! God reigns over the nations; God sits on his holy throne" (RSV). In this and many other Scriptures, God tells us He is the supreme ruler of His universe. (See Psalms 24:1, 46:10, 83:18; 1 Timothy 6:15.)

When the Bible says that God is sovereign it means that He is King of kings and Lord of lords who is actively exercising absolute rule over all His creation. As the sovereign ruler over His universe, God is answerable to none but Himself. He is not obligated to explain His actions to His creatures. He doesn't have to tell us why He does what He does. God is His own reason for all His actions, and whatever God does, He does for His own good pleasure.

Now when we look at the world scene and see the evil that

abounds and the mess we are in because of it, it certainly doesn't seem that God is ruling. It seems that if God is really in charge, then surely He'd be doing a better job of looking after things. I know if I were in charge, I'd straighten things out pretty quick. So we ask ourselves, *How is it that God, who is supposed to be good, can be in charge of a world that is so messed up?*

Most people can't reconcile a good God with a bad world. So they conclude that either there is no God, or if God does exist, He must not be in charge and man is left to his own fate. *The problem with this thinking is that it comes from looking at the world rather than the Word of God.*

When I look at the world, I see a hopeless chaotic mess that is getting worse by the day. And I don't see any way of escape. But when I read the Word of God, I see that there is a God who is behind the scenes moving the course of world events right on schedule. When I begin to look at the world through the eyes of God, I have hope and faith, and rest in the God who is ruling absolutely for His glory and my good. So in this chapter we are going to look at the world through the eyes of God as revealed in the pages of the Bible. We're going to examine four realms of God's sovereignty.

God Is Sovereign Over Nature

The Bible tells us that God exercises His sovereign rule over *nature*. Psalms 135:6-7 reads, "Whatever the LORD pleases he does, in heaven and on earth, in the seas and all deeps. He it is who makes the clouds rise at the end of the earth, who makes lightnings for the rain and brings forth the wind from his storehouses" (RSV).

God created the universe as it pleased Him. He certainly has the right to do as He will with that which He has created. This is the essence of a conversation between God and Job. Job questioned God's justice in dealing with him. God replied to Job from His position as sovereign ruler over nature.

God said to Job, "Where were you when I laid the earth's foundation? Tell me, if you understand. Who marked off its dimensions? Surely you know! Who stretched a measuring line across it? On what were its footings set, or who laid its cornerstone—while the morning stars sang together and all the angels shouted for joy?

"Who shut up the sea behind doors when it burst forth from the womb, when I made the clouds its garment and wrapped it in thick darkness, when I fixed limits for it and set its doors and bars in place, when I said, 'This far you may come and no farther; here is where your proud waves halt'?

"Have you ever given orders to the morning, or shown the dawn its place, that it might take the earth by the edges and shake the wicked out of it? The earth takes shape like clay under a seal; its features stand out like those of a garment. The wicked are denied their light, and their upraised arm is broken.

"Have you journeyed to the springs of the sea or walked in the recesses of the deep? Have the gates of death been shown to you? Have you seen the gates of the shadow of death? Have you comprehended the vast expanses of the earth? Tell me, if you know all this.

"What is the way to the abode of light? And where does darkness reside? Can you take them to their places? Do you know the paths to their dwellings? Surely you know, for you were already born! You have lived so many years!" (Job 38:4-21 NIV).

God continued this line of questioning through the rest of chapters 38 and 39, revealing to Job His sovereign rule over nature. When God finished making His point, all Job could say was, "I am unworthy—how can I reply to you? I put my hand over my mouth. I spoke once, but I have no answer— twice but I will say no more" (Job 40:4-5 NIV).

Yes, God exercises sovereign rule over nature. Now when God created, He set over His creation certain natural laws that give order to that which He created. We call these "laws of nature." Nature obeys the laws that God set over it. So all that God created, except man, operates in an orderly and harmonious manner within the sovereign will of God as it pleases Him.

Even though God is sovereign over that which He has created, He Himself is not limited by His creation. So any time that it pleases Him, God can override His natural laws and perform what we call a miracle.

God demonstrated His sovereignty over creation through the miracles which are recorded in the Bible. For example, He sent plagues in Egypt to force the Pharaoh to let the Hebrews go free. Then He parted the Red Sea for them to make their final escape. For forty years God provided for their every need, even preserving their clothing. When it came time for the Hebrews to enter their land, God divided the waters of the Jordan River. When the Hebrews entered the land, God knocked down the walls of Jericho. On one occasion, God stopped the sun, thereby helping to give Joshua a great victory. As a witness to King Hezekiah, God actually turned back the clock by moving back the shadow of the sundial.

In the days of Jesus, God walked on the water and calmed the seas. He fed five-thousand men, plus women and children, with five loaves of bread and two fish. He healed the sick, opened the eyes of the blind and the ears of the deaf, made the lame to walk and even raised the dead. And to show that He is lord over life and death, He came forth from the grave itself.

Many people today can testify that God is still performing miracles. And in the future, God is going to dramatically demonstrate His sovereign rule over the universe. The Book of Revelation says that God will turn the sun to black and the moon to blood red. He will cast down the stars to earth and roll up the heavens like a scroll. He will burn up a third of the trees and all the grass. He will turn the seas and the rivers to blood, while diminishing light by eight hours. He will dry up the Euphrates River, destroy every city, flatten every mountain, sink every island and drop one-hundred-pound hailstones on those who blaspheme His name. Finally, He will return from the heavens to establish an everlasting kingdom on planet earth. God is sovereign over His creation.

God Is Sovereign Over Individuals

God is also sovereign over His *human creatures*. Proverbs 16:9 reads, "A man's mind plans his way, but the Lord directs his steps" (RSV). A similar statement is made in Proverbs 19:21, "Many are the plans in the mind of a man, but it is the purpose of the LORD that will be established" (RSV).

This brings two questions to our mind. *Since God is sovereign, "Why does He allow sin," and "How can man have a free will?"* These are certainly challenging questions. It seems that the Bible teaches that God allows sin because He has given man a degree of freedom to either choose to obey Him, or choose to rebel against Him. Yet at the same time, God maintains His sovereignty over what man does. Now this sounds like a contradiction. But it isn't. Let me suggest the following solution.

God has absolute freedom, while man has only limited freedom. So we are really talking about degrees of freedom. *Only God is absolutely free.* Only God can do whatever He desires, whenever He desires and nobody and nothing can stop Him. He is able to do as He pleases always, everywhere and forever because He is all power, all knowledge, everywhere present and is limitless, boundless and absolutely free.

Now what human can we say that about? Well, of course, none. Humans have limited freedom. We're limited by time, space, food, water, shelter, mental and physical capacities, life and death, etc. God allows us to live and make choices within the bounds of our limited freedom. But only God is absolutely free. And one of the decisions that God has made is to allow sin. God in His absolute freedom, permits sin out of our limited freedom, knowing in advance that He will judge sin in the "Day of His Wrath." But until that day, the sin that God allows out of our limited freedom cannot go beyond the bounds that God has fixed for it out of His absolute freedom.

We see an example of this between a father and his son. The father, in the son's eyes, has absolute freedom to tell the son what he must do. Dad is in charge as long as the son lives under his roof. He is king of his castle. Yet, at the same time, the father gives the son a certain amount of freedom to make his own decisions. However, both the father and the son understand that there is a limit to the son's freedom. The son must operate within the bounds of his limited freedom. And if the son tries to extend his freedom beyond the bounds that his father has established, then he "pulls in the reins," taking away the son's freedom.

God's sovereignty works with individuals in a similar way. *God, in His absolute freedom, overrules the sin out of our limited freedom and uses it for His own good purposes.* And we humans, blinded by our pride, are not even aware that God is doing it. We think we are pulling one over on God and having our own way. We think we're our own man. We think we're thumbing our nose at God and getting away with it, while all along, God is overriding and offsetting our evil and using it for His own good purposes. God has the final say. *He accomplishes His purposes and uses anyone who happens to be in the way to the working of His will, whether they are aware of it or not.* God overcomes evil for good yet holds the unrepentant evildoer guilty. Men, even in their sins, are still carrying out God's plans.

Now let's look at one example of this in the Bible. It's the story of Joseph. Joseph was his Daddy's favorite. This made his brothers very jealous. At one point they sold Joseph as a slave to the Egyptians. They thought "good riddance to Joseph." But Joseph became a ruler in Egypt. Then, when a famine came to the land, Joseph's brothers went to Egypt for food. While they were there begging for bread, Joseph revealed his identity to them. In doing so, he made the following remarkable statement, "And God sent me before you to preserve for you a remnant on earth, and to keep alive for you many survivors. So it was not you who sent me here, but God . . ." (Genesis 45:7-8 RSV).

Joseph said that God sent him to Egypt. On the surface it looked like evil was winning. But God was behind the scenes, bringing good out of evil. Joseph went on to say, "As for you, you meant evil against me; but God meant it for good . . ." (Genesis 50:20 RSV). What Joseph's brothers meant for evil, God meant for good. We learn from this story that God is moving the course of world events, overriding evil and using it for His glory and the good of those who love Him and are the called according to His purpose (Romans 8:28).

The Apostle James reminds us of this with these words, "Come now, you who say, 'Today or tomorrow we will go into such and such a town and spend a year there and trade and get gain'; whereas you do not know about tomorrow. What is your life? For you are a mist that appears for a little time and then vanishes. Instead you ought to say, 'If the Lord wills, we shall live and we shall do this or that' "(James 4:13-15 RSV).

God Is Sovereign Over His Decree

The third realm of God's sovereignty that we want to discuss relates to His *decree*. God's decree is His purpose for creation. *God has an eternal purpose for His creation with a completed plan that He determined before He laid the foundations of the world.* God has always had the same plan, and He did not have to alter it or put in a last-minute substitute after man sinned. This is because God, knowing everything, allowed for man's sin in His plan.

So God's decree is His eternal purpose for His creation. And to accomplish this eternal purpose God, in His absolute sovereignty, has foreordained as a certainty, all the events of the universe, past, present and future. This means that *the flow of history is simply the unfolding of God's plan to achieve His eternal purpose.*

Now let's look at some places in the Bible where God confirms this. Isaiah 46:8-10 reads, "Remember this and consider, recall it to mind, you transgressors, remember the former things of old; for I am God, and there is no other; I am God and there is none like me, declaring the end from the beginning and from ancient times things not yet done, saying, 'My counsel shall stand, and I will accomplish all of my purpose . . .' "(RSV).

James also recognized this realm of God's sovereignty in Acts 15:18, "Known to God from eternity are all His works" (NKJ). We see, then, that God is working out His eternal decree through the flow of history.

God's decree goes by various names in the Bible. It's called His purpose (Ephesians 1:11; Romans 8:28-29), His counsel or pleasure (Isaiah 46:10; Revelation 4:11) and the counsel of His will (Ephesians 1:11; Daniel 4:35). All of these references to God's decree tell us that God, out of His own absolute free-will, without consulting anyone, has determined to bring about something through His creation according to His own good pleasure. In other words, "God decided to do something just because He wanted to do something." He didn't need to; He chose to just because it was His good pleasure.

Now God does not want us to be ignorant of His decree. He wants us to know why He created us. He wants us to know the purpose for our existence. So He tells us throughout the pages of the Bible. Let's now read some verses where God makes this plain to us.

In Revelation 4:11 we read the following praise to God, "You are worthy, O Lord, To receive glory and honor and power; For You created all things, And by Your will they exist and were created" (NKJ). The old King James Version says God created us for His pleasure. The next question we should ask is, "What is God's pleasure?"

God gives us the answer to this question in Isaiah 43:5-7, "Fear not, for I am with you; I will bring your descendants from the east, And gather you from the west; I will say to the north, 'Give them up!' And to the south, 'Do not keep them back!' Bring My sons from afar, and My daughters from the ends of the earth—Everyone who is called by My name, Whom I have created for My glory; I have formed him, yes, I have made him" (NKJ). In this and many other Scriptures, God says that He made us for His glory. (See 2 Timothy 2:10; 1 Thessalonians 2:12; 1 Peter 5:10.)

God's purpose in creation is to glorify Himself through His creatures. This is why God made us and is our purpose for existing.

But we know that Adam sinned, and when Adam sinned, he lost the glory of God. He was so ashamed that he tried to cover himself with fig leaves. We speak of this tragedy as the "fall of man." But as I said at the beginning of this discussion, Adam's sin did not take God by surprise. God knew that Adam would sin so He made allowances for it in His plan.

God told Adam and Eve that at a certain point in history, He (God) would come into the world to restore His glory to man. This promise is given by God to Adam and Eve in Genesis 3:15. God then moved the flow of history towards this event. Then, at God's appointed time, God prepared for Himself a body and came into the world as the man Jesus Christ. (See Matthew 1:23-25.)

God was to fulfill His purposes through the birth, life, death and resurrection of His Son. Out of man's limited freedom, God allowed Jesus to be crucified. But just so we would know that God was really in charge of it all, Jesus said that no man was going to take His life but that He was going to lay it down of His own free-will (John 10:17-18).

Peter also spoke of this after the resurrection when he preached his great sermon on the day of Pentecost. He said, "Men of Israel, hear these words; Jesus of Nazareth, a Man attested by God to you by miracles, wonders, and signs which God did through Him in your midst, as you yourselves know—Him, being delivered by the determined counsel and foreknowledge of God, you have taken by lawless hands, have crucified, and put to death; whom God raised up, having loosed the pains of death, because it was not possible that He should be held by it" (Acts 2:22-24 NKJ).

So we see that God overruled the evil in man's heart that crucified Jesus by resurrecting Jesus and crowning Him with glory. The writer of Hebrews summarized it in these words, "But we see Jesus, who was made a little lower than the angels, for the suffering of death, crowned with glory and honor, that He, by the grace of God, might taste death for everyone. For it was fitting for Him, for whom are all things and by whom are all things, in bringing many sons to glory, to make the author of their salvation perfect through sufferings" (Hebrews 2:9-10 NKJ).

We see that God's decree, purpose or good pleasure is to bring many sons into glory through Christ Jesus. In John 17:22, Jesus prayed that this decree would become a reality in the lives of His followers. He prayed to God the Father, "And the glory which You gave Me I have given them, that they may be one just as We are one" (NKJ).

By personally appropriating His death and resurrection on our behalf, we can have new life in Jesus Christ and eternal glory with God. Here's how Paul said it to the Romans, "For as many as are led by the Spirit of God, these are the sons of God. For you did not receive the spirit of bondage again to fear, but you received the Spirit of adoption by whom we cry out, 'Abba, Father.' The Spirit Himself bears witness with our spirit that we are children of God, and if children, then heirs—heirs of God and joint heirs with Christ, if indeed we suffer with Him, that we may also be glorified together. For I consider that the sufferings of this present time are not worthy to be compared with the glory which shall be revealed in us" (Romans 8:14-18 NKJ).

Now with this introduction to God's absolute sovereignty and His purpose for us being here, we can better understand these words from Paul, "And we know that all things work together for good to those who love God, to those who are the called according to His purpose, For whom He fore-knew, He also predestined to be conformed to the image of His Son, that He might be the firstborn among many brethren. Moreover whom He predestined, these He also called; whom He called, these He also justified; and whom He justified, these He also glorified" (Romans 8:28-30 NKJ).

God Is Sovereign Over the Flow of History

Now finally we want to consider God's sovereignty over the *flow of history*. We have already read a few verses that revealed this, but now let's look at some more. Psalms 22:28 reads, "For dominion belongs to the LORD, and he rules over the nations" (RSV).

In the Book of Daniel, King Nebuchadnezzar of Babylon

had a terrifying dream. (See Daniel 2:31-45.) He saw a great image of a man. This image had a head of gold, chest and arms of silver, belly and thighs of brass, legs of iron and feet that were part iron and clay. Now Nebuchadnezzar did not understand the meaning of this dream. But God gave the Prophet Daniel the interpretation. God revealed to Daniel that the terrible image represented the Gentile nations that would rule over Israel during the course of world history. These would be evil nations, but God would use them for His glory.

Then Daniel began to worship God for His sovereignty over the nations. He said, ". . . Praise be to the name of God for ever and ever; wisdom and power are his . . . he sets up kings and deposes them . . ." (Daniel 2:19-21 NIV). (See also Daniel 4:17, 24-25, 31-37.)

When God delivered the Hebrews from Egypt, He promised to give them a land of their own. But He said they could only stay in their land as long as they were faithful to God. If they were unfaithful, He would raise up nations and use them as a means of judgment against Israel. Then when that nation had served its purpose, He would destroy it because of its evil and raise up another nation in its place. *This cycle would continue throughout the course of world history until God determined to bring it to a close with the second coming of Jesus Christ.* Let's briefly review the identity of these nations and see how God has been behind the scenes using them for His own good pleasure.

Babylon (606-536 B.C.)

The first nation was Babylon. Daniel told Nebuchadnezzar that the head of gold on the image represented the Babylonian empire (Daniel 2:38). *Under Nebuchadnezzar, much of the whole known world was united in one empire.*

Now before God brought the Hebrews into their land, He told them to let the land rest every seventh year (Leviticus 25:1-7). This was known as the seven year Sabbath. However, for 490 years the Hebrews disobeyed this command, and sinned in other ways as well. Therefore, God raised up Babylon as a world power and allowed the Babylonians to conquer Jerusalem and take the Hebrews captive. They were to be captive seventy years, one year for each seven year Sabbath which they did not keep. (See 2 Chronicles 36:14-21.) After God's holy anger had been fully vindicated and the seventy years were over, God no longer needed Nebuchadnezzar. It was time for the Hebrews to go back home.

Medo-Persia (536-333 B.C.)

God then raised up the Medo-Persian empire and used King Cyrus as His instrument for *freeing the Hebrews* from Babylonian captivity and allowing them to return to their homeland. (See 2 Chronicles 36:22-23.) The chest and arms of silver on the image represented the Medo-Persian empire (Daniel 2:39, 5:22-31, 8:1-4, 20).

Greece (333-323 B.C.)

When God was through with Cyrus, He raised up Alexander the Great and established Greece as the third great Gentile power. The Greek empire was represented on the image by the belly and thighs of brass (Daniel 2:39, 8:5-8, 21). *God used Alexander to establish the Greek language as the universal language of the world which God would use in writing the Gospel of Jesus Christ and the complete New Testament.* And since Greek had already been established as the universal language of the day, everyone would be able to read the Gospels. Once Alexander had accomplished this task, the Greek empire was no longer important. So Alexander died at an early age and his generals fought over the empire until the Greek language was common throughout the known world.

Rome (30 B.C.-A.D. 364)

When God was through with Greece, He raised up the Romans. The Roman empire was represented on the image by the legs of iron (Daniel 2:40, 9:26). The Romans were the great road builders. *God used the Romans to build the roads to carry the Gospel in the Greek language to the united empire originally established in Babylon.* Isn't that amazing?

John records the following conversation between Jesus and Pilate, the Roman governor, " 'Do you refuse to speak to me?' Pilate said. 'Don't you realize I have power either to free you or to crucify you?' Jesus answered, 'You would have no power over me if it were not given to you from above . . . ' " (John 19:10-11 NIV). This was a clear statement by Jesus regarding the sovereignty of God over the Roman empire. Although Rome cooperated with the Jews in crucifying Jesus, God has the final word. For in A.D. 312, Christianity became the official religion of Rome.

The Revived Roman Empire

When the Roman empire had fulfilled its purpose, God divided it into the great colonial powers of the world which were eventually further divided into the modern states of Europe. *God did not completely destroy the Roman empire, but He divided it, holding it in reserve until the last days when He would unite it once again.* (See Daniel 2:41.)

The AntiChrist

The Bible teaches that God plans to revive the Roman empire in the last days and unite it under one last world ruler whom the Bible calls "The AntiChrist." He will rule over a ten-nation confederacy which is represented on the image by the ten toes of iron and clay (Daniel 2:41-43, 9:27).

The AntiChrist represents the ultimate of man seeking his own sovereignty. The ten nations in the revived Roman empire will give him their allegiance, thinking that this is their own doing. But we read in Revelation 17:17, "For God has put it into their hearts to fulfill His purpose, to be of one mind, and to give their kingdom to the beast, until the words of God are fulfilled" (NKJ).

So we see that even this final attempt by man to rule the world is allowed by God. The purpose of this is to bring the nations together for the battle of Armageddon and the second coming of Jesus Christ. This is why God allows the

AntiChrist to rise to power and unite the ten-nation confederacy.

Christ the Smiting Stone

In Luke 21:24 Jesus spoke of this entire period of Gentile domination of Israel as the "Times of the Gentiles." It began with Babylon and will end with the second coming of Jesus Christ to planet earth. Nebuchadnezzar also saw this in his dream. *The coming kingdom of Christ was presented as a stone that would destroy the image by smashing it at its feet.* This caused the whole image to crumble, and the stone grew to become a great mountain that covered the earth. Daniel interpreted this to be a reference to the second coming of Jesus Christ, at which time, He would destroy the Anti-Christ at the battle of Armageddon and put an end to Gentile domination of Israel. (See Daniel 2:34-35, 44-45, 7:13-14.) The fulfillment of this is recorded in Revelation 19:11-21.

This is certainly not an exhaustive study of the subject; there are many more Scriptures which we could study that demonstrate the sovereignty of God. However, I believe we have considered enough Scriptures to clearly see this teaching in the Bible. God is sovereign. He is sovereign over nature. He is sovereign over individuals. He is sovereign over His decree. He is sovereign over the flow of history. It is my prayer that you will recognize His sovereign rule and Lordship in every area of your life. If there is something in your life that you have not turned over to Him, please do so now. You'll be glad you did.

Chapter 6—God Is Sovereign

Review Exercise 5

1. Define the meaning of the word "sovereign" as it applies to God.

2. List the four realms of God's sovereignty and briefly state how God exercises His sovereignty over each.

    a.

    b.

    c.

    d.

3. How can you apply this knowledge to your life?

7

God Is All Power

We have just learned that the living God is the absolute Lord and ruler over all He has created. Now in order to rule, one must have power. In order to rule absolutely, one must have absolute power. So as a follow-up to God's sovereignty we now want to see what the Bible says about God's power.

God's Almighty Power

In the Book of Revelation we read, "And I heard, as it were, the voice of a great multitude, as the sound of many waters and as the sound of mighty thunderings, saying, 'Alleluia! For the Lord God Omnipotent reigns'" (Revelation 19:6 NKJ).

In this verse, John connects God's reign, or rule, with His power. He uses the word "omnipotent" to describe God's power. The word omnipotent means almighty, or all-powerful. And John says that God rules as the almighty, all-powerful one.

God alone is almighty. He alone has absolute power. In this scene, John sees the heavenly host worshiping God for this attribute of power. We learned in an earlier chapter, and it's good to be reminded, God's attributes are biblical revelations about God Himself. Therefore, the truths presented about God are not things He possesses but who God is in Himself. The idea is not so much that God has power, but that God is power.

God is power, and all power comes from Him. *Every expression of power in the universe comes from God who by nature is all-powerful.* We learn this from Psalms 62:11 which says, ". . . power belongs to God" (RSV).

It seems almost silly to point out, but we humans do not have all power. We get frustrated because we do not have the power to do all that we desire. I will to do certain things, but I do not have the power to do them. But you know God never gets frustrated. God never wishes. For God to will is for God to do. Abraham learned this lesson and said, "Is anything too hard for the LORD?" (Genesis 18:14 NKJ). Of course Abraham was not asking a question but stating a fact about God which he had observed.

God's Power and Knowledge
With God's all knowledge, He knows all things. With His all power, He is able to do all that He knows. But God will only do that which is consistent with His being. *God never does anything that will contradict Himself.* He cannot exercise one of His attributes at the expense of any of His other attributes. That would be going against His nature.

Foolish people often ask, "Can God make a rock so big that He couldn't lift it?" Well, certainly He could out of His absolute power. But His absolute power is balanced by His absolute knowledge. He could, but He won't because He can't.

God's Power Is Balanced
Neither can God use His power in violation of His moral character of perfect love, justice, holiness and goodness.

Those who know God's love in Jesus Christ need not fear His power. This is because God always exercises His power towards Christians for their good. We can find rest in this kind of God because we need not be afraid of Him.

On the contrary, for those who live in sin, God cannot restrain His power forever. His perfect holiness and justice demand that His power be executed in the form of wrath and judgment against all ungodliness. Paul writes in Romans 1:18, "For the wrath of God is revealed from heaven against all ungodliness and wickedness of men who by their wickedness suppress the truth" (RSV).

Now God is longsuffering and not willing that any should perish (2 Peter 2:3). But in the final judgment, those who have rejected His mercy through Jesus Christ will incur His wrath (Revelation 6:15-17). In contrast to Christians, unredeemed sinners should fear God's power, although His first desire is to use His power for our good.

God's Power Is Eternal

In an earlier chapter, we learned that God is eternal. This means that He transcends, or is outside of, time. Now since God is eternal, all that He is in Himself (His attributes) is eternal. Therefore, His power is eternal.

There's a passage in the Book of Revelation that links God's power to His eternal being. It reads, " 'I am the Alpha and the Omega, the Beginning and the End,' says the Lord, 'who is and who was and who is to come, the Almighty' " (Revelation 1:8 NKJ). Here we learn that God is the eternal all-powerful One. This means that God never gets tired. He never gets out of breath. He never has to take a break. He never has to recharge His battery, because He never runs down. *He always was all power, always is all power, and always will be all power.*

On the contrary, when we humans exert just a little bit of energy, we get out of breath and have to stop and rest. This is because when we use power, we lose power. We have to continually build ourselves back up to normal strength.

But since God is eternal in His power, whatever acts of

73

power He has done in the past, He can still do today. Whatever He does today, He will be able to do tomorrow. Many Christians do not realize this eternal aspect of God's power. They think God used to do things, "way back then," but that He doesn't do anything now. But this is impossible because there's no "way back then" for God. He is outside of time.

The Prophet Isaiah spoke of God's eternal power with these words, "Have you not known? Have you not heard? The LORD is the everlasting God, the Creator of the ends of the earth. He does not faint or grow weary, his understanding is unsearchable. He gives power to the faint, and to him who has no might he increases strength" (Isaiah 40:28-29 RSV).

Since God is eternal, He is the same yesterday, today and forever. So we need to understand that when the Bible says that God rested on the seventh day (Genesis 2:2), it wasn't because He was tired. It was because He was through. The eternal all-powerful God can still deliver you from the fiery furnaces of life today, just as He did "then."

God's Power Is Infinite

God's power is also infinite. We have learned that infinite means limitless, boundless, measureless. This tells us that *God can do anything as easily as anything else.*

For example, let's say there are three Christians with three different financial needs. One Christian needs $500, the second Christian needs $5,000 and the third Christian needs $50,000. God can supply the third Christian with the $50,000 just as easily as He can the first Christian with the $500.

God has no limits, so we should not limit Him in our expections of Him. Our thoughts of God are too small. We have an infinite all-powerful God. Let's put Him to the test. As we walk with God, let's ask Him for big things and expect big things from Him.

God not only says that He is all power, but He has proven this to be true through mighty acts in which He has manifested His power. We are now going to examine five ways God has manifested His power to us.

74

God's Power in Creation

The first way God has manifested His power to us is through *creation*. When man creates something, he must have some kind of matter or material from which to work. Man cannot make something out of nothing. Technically speaking, man doesn't create anything, he just rearranges what God has already created.

God, on the other hand, begins with nothing. Genesis 1 tells us that God spoke the world into existence. God said "Light be" and there was light. He said "Firmament (sky) be" and there was sky. He said "Earth be" and there was earth. With one word, God spoke the entire solar system into being. With one word, He filled the oceans with fish, the air with birds, the earth with every kind of animal. Then God spoke once again and the breath of life came out of Him who is life and man became a living soul.

Psalms 33:6-9 reads, "By the word of the LORD the heavens were made, and all their host by the breath of his mouth. He gathered the waters of the sea as in a bottle; he put the deeps in storehouses. Let all the earth fear the LORD, let all the inhabitants of the world stand in awe of him! For he spoke, and it came to be; he commanded and it stood forth" (RSV).

In Job 26:7 it says that God, "hangs the earth upon nothing" (RSV).

The Prophet Jeremiah wrote, ". . . 'These gods, who did not make the heavens and the earth, will perish from the earth and from under the heavens.' But God made the earth by his power; he founded the world by his wisdom and stretched out the heavens by his understanding. When he thunders, the waters in the heavens roar; he makes clouds rise from the ends of the earth. He sends lightning with the rain and brings out the wind from his storehouses.

"Everyone is senseless and without knowledge; every goldsmith is shamed by his idols. His images are a fraud; they have no breath in them. They are worthless, the objects of mockery; when their judgment comes, they will perish. He who is the Portion of Jacob is not like these, for he is the Maker of all things, including Israel, the tribe of his inheritance—the LORD Almighty is his name" (Jeremiah 10:11-16 NIV).

Whatever God wills to be, He speaks into existence out of His almighty power. So that out of God's power, His spoken word produces something where there was nothing. Hebrews 11:3 puts it this way, "By faith we understand that the worlds were framed by the word of God, so that the things which are seen were not made of things which are visible" (NKJ). The scientific community can search to the ends of the earth looking for evidence of the origin of creation. But they are not going to find it because God Himself is the origin. The creator God is the source of all life and we live and move and have our being in Him.

God Preserves His Creation

Not only did God create out of His power through His spoken word, but in the same way, He preserves that which He has created. Hebrews 1:3 tells us that Jesus, who as the eternal Son of God, participated in creation and holds the universe together by the word of His power. Paul wrote that by Jesus all things consist (Colossians 1:17).

God brings things about in His universe by His spoken word (Psalms 29). In Job 38:23, God told Job that He was storing up the hail for the last days to rain it down from the heaven in the day of battle and war. Job responded, "I know that you can do all things; no plan of yours can be thwarted" (Job 42:2 NIV). We see the fulfillment of this statement in Revelation 16:21, when out of God's power, His spoken word sends forth one-hundred-pound hailstones to fall upon men who blaspheme His name in preparation for the second coming of Jesus.

Speaking of the second coming of Jesus Christ, Isaiah writes, "But with righteousness He shall judge the poor, And decide with equity for the meek of the earth; He shall strike the earth with the rod of His mouth, and with the breath of His lips He shall slay the wicked" (Isaiah 11:4 NKJ).

Paul writes in 2 Thessalonians 2:8, "And then the lawless one will be revealed, whom the Lord will consume with the breath of His mouth and destroy with the brightness of His coming" (NKJ).

We see the fulfillment of these verses in Revelation 19:15, "Now out of His mouth goes a sharp sword, that with it He should strike the nations . . ." (NKJ).

Yes, God has created and is preserving His universe out of His almighty power. But even this work of God only gives us a tiny glimpse of God's power. God has infinitely more power than He has revealed to us in His universe. Speaking of God's creation, Job said, "And these are but the outer fringe of his works; how faint the whisper we hear of him!" (Job 26:14 NIV). Therefore, God has revealed His power to us in other ways.

God's Power in Becoming One of Us

The second way God has revealed His power to us is *by becoming one of us.* Luke records the following conversation between the angel Gabriel and Mary, "Then the angel said to her, 'Do not be afraid, Mary, for you have found favor with God. And behold, you will conceive in your womb and bring forth a Son, and shall call His name JESUS. He will be great, and will be called the Son of the Highest; and the Lord God will give Him the throne of His father David. And He will reign over the house of Jacob forever, and of His kingdom there will be no end.' Then Mary said to the angel, 'How can this be, since I do not know a man?' And the angel answered and said to her, 'The Holy Spirit will come upon you, and the power of the Highest will overshadow you; therefore, also, that Holy One who is to be born will be called the Son of God. For with God nothing will be impossible' " (Luke 1:30-35, 37 NKJ).

Now why was it necessary for God to do this? Because all of us have sinned and come short of the glory of God. All we like sheep have gone astray. We've turned to our own way rather than God's way. There is none righteous before God. The penalty for our sin is death. The wrath of God's violated justice must be satisfied. (See Isaiah 53; Romans 3:10-25, 6:23.)

77

But God also loves us. He wants to save us from our sins. Yet God cannot exercise His love at the expense of His justice. So He devised a plan to save us that would satisfy and be consistent with Himself. *God's plan says, "Even though the penalty for sin is death, you don't have to pay it. I'll come to earth and pay it for you."*

You see, God couldn't save us way up there in the high and holy place. God couldn't save us in heaven, because God is a spirit, and a spirit does not have flesh and blood. Yet blood is the evidence that the penalty has been paid, and without the shedding of blood there is no forgiveness of sin.

Therefore, God prepared for Himself a body and became one of us. The creator became one of the creatures. The Master became the servant. The Son of God became the Son of man and the Lord of glory became a baby in a manger. He was known as Emmanuel, which we have already learned means God with us. They called Him Jesus of Nazareth. (See Matthew 1:23-25.)

Jesus was the Lamb of God who had come to take away the sins of the world. He would be the once and for all perfect sacrifice so that no more sacrifices would be needed. The writer of Hebrews puts it this way, ". . . it is impossible for the blood of bulls and goats to take away sins. Therefore, when Christ came into the world, He said, 'Sacrifice and offering you did not desire, but a body you prepared for me; with burnt offerings and sin offerings you were not pleased. Then I said, "Here I am—it is written about me in the scroll—I have come to do your will, O God." '

"First he said, 'Sacrifice and offerings, burnt offerings and sin offerings you did not desire, nor were you pleased with them'(although the law required them to be made). Then he said, 'Here I am, I have come to do your will.' He sets aside the first to establish the second. And by that will, we have been made holy through the sacrifice of the body of Jesus Christ once and for all" (Hebrews 10:4-10 NIV).

God the Father stayed on the throne to rule the universe. God the Son came into the world to save the universe. God the Holy Spirit prepared a womb to receive Him. The power

*of the Most High overshadowed Mary, and out of God's
power, the word became flesh.*

Jesus was born supernaturally of a virgin. This was
necessary in order that Jesus would not inherit man's sin
nature passed down from Adam. So Jesus was born of the
"seed of woman," not the seed of man. God brought it about
out of his His power. Jesus proved Himself to be God by His
mighty acts of power. He made the blind to see, the lame to
walk, and the deaf to hear. He exercised authority over
demons, multiplied the bread and fish, walked on the water
and calmed the seas. He healed the leper, restored the
withered hand and raised the dead.

*He said that all power had been given to Him in heaven
and earth* (Matthew 28:18). He lived a perfect life and never
sinned. But it was necesary for Him to die that we might live.
So they crucified Him. He could have called down thousands
of angels (Matthew 26:53) but He stayed on the cross. At
noon, God the Father blackened the sun and covered the
whole world with darkness. Then Jesus said, "It is finished"
and dismissed His spirit (John 19:30). They took His body
down and buried Him.

God's Power Over Life and Death

But God didn't end the story there. There was more of His
power about which He wanted us to know. So three days
later, when the women went to anoint Jesus' body with oil,
they were met by an angel. The angel said to the women, "Do
not be afraid, for I know that you seek Jesus who was
crucified. He is not here; For He is risen . . ." (Matthew
28:5-6 NKJ). So thirdly, through the resurrection of Jesus
Christ, God has shown us that He has *power over life and
death.*

Jesus had earlier said, "Therefore My Father loves Me,
because I lay down My life that I may take it again. No one
takes it from Me, but I lay it down of Myself. I have power to
lay it down, and I have power to take it again" (John
10:17-18 NKJ).

He said on another occasion, ". . . I am the resurrection

and the life. He who believes in Me, though he may die, he shall live. And whoever lives and believes in Me shall never die" (John 11:25-26 NKJ).

Paul writes in 1 Corinthians 15:20-26, "But now Christ is risen from the dead, and has become the firstfruits of those who have fallen asleep. For since by man came death, by Man also came the resurrection of the dead. For as in Adam all die, even so in Christ all shall be made alive. But each one in his own order: Christ the firstfruits, afterward those who are Christ's at His coming. Then comes the end, when He delivers the kingdom to God the Father, when He puts an end to all rule and all authority and power. For He must reign till He has put all enemies under His feet. The last enemy that will be destroyed is death" (NKJ).

God's Power in Saving Us

Fourth, God has shown us His power in *saving us from our sins.* Jesus told His disciples, ". . . 'Assuredly, I say to you that it is hard for a rich man to enter the kingdom of heaven. And again I say to you, it is easier for a camel to go through the eye of a needle than for a rich man to enter the kingdom of God.' When His disciples heard it, they were exceedingly amazed, saying, 'Who then can be saved?' But Jesus looked at them and said to them, 'With men this is impossible, but with God all things are possible' "(Matthew 19:23-26 NKJ).

With these words, Jesus was saying that it is impossible for man to save himself. Our good works cannot save us. Being religious cannot save us. We cannot buy our way into heaven. None of the things we try to do to earn our way into heaven are acceptable to God. Therefore, man cannot save himself.

But with God, all things are possible. "For God so loved the world that He gave His only begotten Son, that whoever believes in Him should not perish but have everlasting life. For God did not send His Son into the world to condemn the world, but that the world through Him might be saved" (John 3:16-17 NKJ).

Paul writes to the Romans, ". . . If you confess with your mouth the Lord Jesus and believe in your heart that God has raised Him from the dead, you will be saved. For with the heart one believes to righteousness, and with the mouth confession is made to salvation. For the Scripture says, 'Whoever calls upon the name of the Lord shall be saved' " (Romans 10:9-13 NKJ).

God's Power in Keeping Us

Finally, God shows us His power by *keeping those whom He has saved.* God is not only able to save us, but He is also able to keep us.

Jesus said in John 10:27-30, "My sheep hear My voice, and I know them, and they follow Me. And I give them eternal life, and they shall never perish: neither shall anyone snatch them out of My hand. My Father, who has given them to Me, is greater than all; and no one is able to snatch them out of My Father's hand. I and My Father are one" (NKJ).

Peter wrote, "Blessed be the God and Father of our Lord Jesus Christ, who according to His abundant mercy has begotten us again to a living hope through the resurrection of Jesus Christ from the dead, to an inheritance incorruptible and undefiled and that does not fade away, reserved in heaven for you, who are kept by the power of God through faith for salvation ready to be revealed in the last time" (1 Peter 1:3-5 NKJ).

We read in Jude, "Now to Him who is able to keep you from stumbling, And to present you faultless Before the presence of His glory with exceeding joy, To God our Savior, Who alone is wise, Be glory and majesty, Dominion and power, Both now and forever. Amen" (Jude 24-25 NKJ).

Paul spoke of the keeping power of God with these words, "What then shall we say to these things? If God is for us, who can be against us? He who did not spare His own Son, but delivered Him up for us all, how shall he not with Him also freely give us all things? Who shall bring a charge against God's elect? It is God who justifies. Who is he who condemns? It is Christ who died, and furthermore is also risen, who is even at the right hand of God, who also makes intercession for us. Who shall separate us from the love of Christ? Shall tribulation, or distress, or persecution, or famine, or nakedness, or peril, or sword? As it is written: 'For your sake we are killed all day long; We are accounted as sheep for the slaughter.' Yet in all these things we are more than conquerors through Him who loved us. For I am persuaded that neither death nor life, nor angels nor principalities nor powers, nor things present nor things to come, nor height nor depth, nor any other created thing, shall be able to separate us from the love of God which is in Christ Jesus our Lord" (Romans 8:31-39 NKJ).

What a way for Paul to end a discussion of God's power. *If God is for us, who can be against us? The answer of course, is no one. God has made all things out of His almighty power and He's preserving it out of the same power.* He rules over life and death so that we live and move and have our being in Him. He is able to save us from our sins, if we will come to Him through Jesus Christ. But He's also able to forever banish us from His presence, if we reject Him. If you don't know Him, come to Him now. For those who do know Him, do not fear that He will lose you, but worship Him for His almighty power and call upon Him in your time of need. *For there is nothing too hard for God.*

Chapter 7—God Is All Power

Review Exercise 6

1. Give your own definition of God's all power.

2. List five ways God has manifested His power to us.

   a.

   b.

   c.

   d.

   e.

3. How can you apply this knowlege to your life?

8

God Is All Knowledge

God is not only all-powerful, but He is also all-knowing. Because God is all-knowing, He is always able to exercise His power consistent with His being. In 1 John 3:20 we read, "For if our heart condemns us, God is greater than our heart, and knows all things" (NKJ). As a follow-up to God's all-power, we're now going to discover what the Bible says about God's all-knowledge.

God's All Knowledge

God is able to rule absolutely and exercise His power consistent with His being because He knows all things. God knows all things because He Himself is all-knowing. As we've mentioned before, knowledge is not something God has, but it is who He is in Himself. Every piece of knowledge in the universe comes from God who by nature is all knowledge.

Now we humans don't know everything. Some folks act

like they do, **but** we all know they don't. We sometimes make bad decisions because we seldom have all the information we need to make the right decision. Our decisions are based on limited knowledge. This is why oil companies, for example, drill more dry holes than they do productive ones. Sometimes, after making a decision, we come across new information that we didn't have at the time we made our decision. And we say, "Oh, if I had only known this, I would have done things differently. I would have made a different decision." The universal remorse of all humans is, "I wish I had known then what I know now; I would have done things differently."

Well, God does not have this problem of not having enough information because He Himself is perfect knowledge (Job 37:16). God never has to have a committee meeting. He never has to call in a specialist. He never has to wait for further developments or "hope" that He did the right thing. There is no wishful thinking with God because He knows everything.

The Prophet Isaiah spoke of God's all-knowledge in these words, "Who has directed the Spirit of the Lord, or as his counselor has instructed him? Whom did he consult for his enlightenment, and who taught him the path of justice, and taught him knowledge, and showed him the way of understanding?" (Isaiah 40:13-14 RSV). Of course, the answer to Isaiah's question is "no one." God doesn't need anyone to instruct Him because He knows everything.

With God's all knowledge, He moves the course of the world events for His glory, the good of His children and the destruction of those who reject Him. This can be very comforting or very disturbing. If you have received God's salvation message in Jesus Christ, you can find rest in a God who knows everything that is taking place and is bringing it to pass out of His sovereign will and power for your good. Now that's comforting. However, if you reject God's salvation message in Jesus Christ, you should know that God is moving the course of world events to bring about your destruction. That's disturbing.

God's Knowledge Is Eternal

God's knowledge is eternal because He is eternal. He is the eternal all-knowing one. This means that what God knows, He's always known. There never was a time when God didn't know everything. *God knows all things that were (past), all things that are (present) and all things that will be (future).* And because God is outside of time, He knows it all instantly. God knows the beginning and the end all at once. James mentions this in Acts 15:18, "Known to God from eternity are all His works" (NKJ). (See also Isaiah 46:8-10.)

Unlike God, we humans are often surprised by events that happen to us. Things don't always work out just the way we thought. We don't know what is just around the corner. We can be deceived. Our plans can be hindered or changed. For example, no one plans a flat tire. And so we're constantly kept just a little off balance because we "don't know."

But now let me give you some encouraging news. God is never off balance. No one can hinder or change His plans. God knows! In Isaiah 66:18, God says, "For I know their works and their thoughts. It shall be that I will gather all nations and tongues; and they shall come and see My glory" (NKJ).

God's Knowledge Is Infinite

God's knowledge is also infinite while ours is finite. We're always having to learn things. We accumulate knowledge over a period of time. Sometimes we even lose part of our storehouse of knowledge by forgetting things which we have learned. What we know is always changing. We know some things better than we do others. I know a lot about a few things, a little about many things but I don't know anything about most things. We do not have equal knowledge of different things. Because we're finite creatures, we're always adding and taking away from our knowledge.

But God is different. There's no adding or taking away of His knowledge. He knows nothing better than anything else but knows everything equally. *In other words, God is an expert on everything.* He never discovers, is never surprised, never amazed, never wonders and is never caught off guard. God does not need to consult an encyclopedia because there's nothing for Him to learn. Putting it in modern terminology, God is a "know-it-all."

God not only knows everything that was (did happen), He also knows everything that might have been but wasn't (did not happen). He not only knows everything that is (now happening), He knows everything that can be but isn't (not now happening). He not only knows everything that will be (will happen), He knows everything that could be but won't be (will not happen).

God knows all that can be known, and He knows it instantly. He knows every possible item of knowledge concerning everything that could have existed, does exist or might exist anywhere in the universe, past, present and future. In other words, God knows all the possibilities. And He's chosen certain ones to take place out of the good pleasure of His sovereign will.

This means that God knows about our little problems as well as our big ones. You have probably said to yourself many times, "Well, God is so busy running the universe that I don't want to bother Him with my little problem." And instead of giving that problem to God, you tried to cope with it yourself. But, you see, for God there is no such thing as a big problem and a little problem. God knows all things equally well. No one has ever had as many problems as Job. Yet Job took comfort in God's all knowledge. He said, "For His eyes are on the ways of man, and He sees all his steps" (Job 34:21 NKJ). We are now going to see four ways in which God's all knowledge affects our lives.

God Knows Himself

First of all, *God knows Himself.* When God told Moses He was the "I Am," He made the greatest declaration of self-awareness the world has ever known.

Man, on the other hand, does not know himself. The Prophet Jeremiah wrote, "The heart is deceitful above all things, And desperately wicked; Who can know it?"

(Jeremiah 17:9 NKJ). **We don't know our** own heart. We like to think we do but experience proves that Jeremiah was speaking the truth. We think we know how we'll react to a given situation, but we really don't. We're always surprising ourselves, aren't we?

But unlike us, God perfectly knows Himself. *He always knows how He is going to act in a given situation.* So He never surprises Himself. He never does anything in such a way that He's later sorry about and wished He'd done things differently. We often strike out against someone and say a harsh word in a moment of anger. Later we're sorry for our actions and words. This would never happen with God.

God always deals with His creatures in a way that is consistent with His being. All of His actions towards us are consistent with His perfect holiness, love, justice and goodness. This is why there has to be a heaven and a hell. Because of our sins, God's holiness and justice demands a hell. But God's love and goodness offers a heaven. *We can find rest in a God who is always going to act towards us out of His perfect knowledge of His perfect moral attributes.*

God Knows What He Is Doing

The second way in which God's perfect knowledge affects our lives is that *God knows what He's doing.* Now it may sound silly to make a statement like this about God. But let me ask you a question. Do you know what you are doing? Do you know your purpose and goal in life and exactly how to go about achieving that goal?

Well, of course, the answer is no! None of us do. Most people just drift along with no idea of what they are doing, or why. Some think they know what they want to do but don't know how to go about doing whatever it is they think they want to do.

Sometimes our goals change. For example, most little boys want to be firemen when they grow up, or maybe astronauts. As they grow up they change their goals. And their plans change. We all make mistakes along the way, and there's no guarantee that we will ever reach our goal. If we are real honest, we must admit that a great deal of the time, we don't have any idea what we are doing.

But God is different. Out of His perfect knowledge, God knows exactly what He wants to do and exactly how to go about doing it in a holy, loving, just, good way. God has always had the same purpose and the same plan. He's always known it and how to execute it and He has never had to change it. God doesn't need a "plan B" just in case His first plan doesn't work out.

In an earlier chapter we learned that God's purpose is His decree. We also learned that God's purpose or decree is to share His glory with all who will come to Him through Jesus Christ. Paul said it this way, "For he chose us in him before the creation of the world to be holy and blameless in his sight. In love he predestined us to be adopted as his sons through Jesus Christ, in accordance with his pleasure and will . . ." (Ephesians 1:4-5 NIV).

Paul also writes in Ephesians 2:10, "For we are God's workmanship, created in Christ Jesus to do good works, which God prepared in advance for us to do" (NIV).

Paul once again writes this same truth to Timothy, "who has saved us and called us to a holy life—not because of anything we have done but because of his own purpose and grace. This grace was given us in Christ Jesus before the beginning of time, but it has now been revealed through the appearance of our Savior, Christ Jesus, who has destroyed death and has brought life and immortality to light through the gospel" (2 Timothy 1:9-10 NIV).

These Scriptures, along with many others, tell us that God has always had the same purpose and plan even before the foundations of the world. God's purpose and plan is centered in Jesus Christ. And at a certain point in time and history, God executed His plan by becoming one of us in order to redeem us and reconcile us to Himself.

Peter expressed this in the following statement, ". . . You know that you were not redeemed with corruptible things, like silver or gold, from your aimless conduct received by traditions from your fathers, but with the precious blood of

Christ, as of a lamb without blemish and without spot. He indeed was foreordained before the foundation of the world, but was manifest in these last times for you who through Him believe in God, who raised Him from the dead and gave Him glory, so that your faith and hope are in God" (1 Peter 1:18-21 NKJ).

Paul spoke of the certainty of God's purpose and plan when he wrote to the Christians in Thessalonica. He said, "Now may the God of peace Himself sanctify you completely; and may your whole spirit, soul, and body be preserved blameless at the coming of our Lord Jesus Christ. He who calls you is faithful, who also will do it" (1 Thessalonians 5:23-24 NKJ).

God Knows the Flow of History

Thirdly, God knows the *flow of history*. Since world history is simply the outworking of God's plan, He obviously knows everything that is going to happen. We earlier referred to Isaiah 46:8-10 which reads, "Remember this and consider, recall it to mind, you transgressors, remember the former things of old; for I am God, and there is no other; I am God, and there is none like me, declaring the end from the beginning and from ancient times things not yet done, saying, 'My counsel shall stand, and I will accomplish all my purpose' " (RSV).

God knew Adam and Eve would sin so He already arranged to clothe them with animal skins as a covering for their sins. Then He promised them that at a certain point in time, He would come to the earth and take their sins away. He told Noah that He would come through his son Shem. He said to Abraham that He would come through Isaac. He revealed to Isaac that He would come through the tribe of Judah. Then He narrowed it down to the family of Jesse. And out of the family of Jesse, God chose David as the kingly lineage through which He would come into the world.

God then raised up prophets to tell more about His coming. God spoke through the prophets telling when He would be born, where He would be born, how He would live, the things He would say and do and even how He would die.

Paul summarizes all of this for us in Galatians 4:4-6, "But when the fullness of the time had come, God sent forth His Son, born of a woman, born under the law, to redeem those who were under the law, that we might receive the adoption as sons. And because you are sons, God has sent forth the Spirit of His Son into your hearts, crying out, 'Abba, Father!' Therefore you are no longer a servant but a son, and if a son, then an heir of God through Christ" (NKJ).

Jesus lived a perfect life and died for our sins. But after three days, He came forth from the grave, victorious over death. He walked planet earth for forty days and nights appearing to over five hundred people. Then He ascended back into heaven from where He came.

As Jesus ascended, two angels appeared to His disciples and said, ". . . Men of Galilee, why do you stand gazing up into heaven? This same Jesus, who was taken up from you into heaven, will so come in like manner as you saw him go into heaven" (Acts 1:11 NKJ).

Jesus said, "Let not your heart be troubled; you believe in God, believe also in Me. In My Father's house are many mansions; if it were not so, I would have told you. I go to prepare a place for you. And if I go and prepare a place for you, I will come again and receive you to Myself; that where I am, there you may be also" (John 14:1-3 NKJ).

Jesus said that He will come again. From the time of His resurrection and ascension, God the Father has been moving the flow of history towards the second coming of Jesus Christ. And from the signs of the times, it appears that His coming just might be closer than we imagine. It just might be that God is going to soon bring an end to the present period of history as we know it and usher in a new age with the second coming of Jesus. Are you prepared to receive Him?

God Knows His Creatures

Finally, God knows His *creatures*. Psalms 147:4-5 reads, "He counts the number of the stars; He calls them all by name. Great is our Lord, and mighty in power; His understanding is infinite" (NKJ). God says in Psalms 50:10-11, "For every beast of the forest is Mine, and the cattle on a thousand hills. I know all the birds of the mountains, and the wild beasts of the field are Mine" (NKJ). Jesus said in Matthew 10:29 that not one sparrow falls to the ground without God knowing about it.

So if God knows His creatures, that means He knows us. Why, He knows us so well, Jesus said that God knows the number of hairs on our head (Matthew 10:30). David wrote these words in Psalms 139:1-5, "O LORD, you have searched me and you know me. You know when I sit and when I rise; you perceive my thoughts from afar. You discern my going out and my lying down; you are familiar with all my ways. Before a word is on my tongue you know it completely, O LORD. You hem me in—behind and before; you have laid your hand upon me" (NIV).

Yes, God knows everything about us. *He knows the things we did in the past; He knows the things we're doing now, and He knows the things we're going to do.* Proverbs 5:21 says, "For the ways of man are before the eyes of the LORD, And He ponders all his paths" (NKJ). The same truth is also taught in Proverbs 15:3, "The eyes of the LORD are in every place, Keeping watch on the evil and the good" (NKJ).

Not only does God know the things we say and do, but He also knows what we'd like to say and what we'd like to do. In other words, God knows every thought that has ever crossed your mind, that is in your mind right at this moment, and every thought you are going to have in the future. God expressed this truth through the Prophet Ezekiel, ". . . I know the things that come into your mind" (Ezekiel 11:5 NKJ).

God not only knows what's in our mind, but He also knows what is in our heart. Proverbs 16:2 reads, "All the ways of a man are pure in his own eyes, but the LORD weighs the spirit" (RSV). God told Samuel, ". . . Man looks on the outward appearance, but the Lord looks on the heart" (1 Samuel 16:7 RSV).

You see, God knows the motive behind everything we do and say and think. We can fool other people; we can even fool ourselves. *But we cannot fool God.* As we just learned from the Prophet Jeremiah, "The heart is deceitful above all things, And desperately wicked; Who can know it? I, the LORD, search the heart, I test the mind, Even to give every man according to his ways, And according to the fruit of his doings" (Jeremiah 17:9-10 NKJ).

We read the same thought in Hebrews 4:12-13, "For the word of God is living and active. Sharper than any double-edged sword, it penetrates even to dividing soul and spirit, joints and marrow; it judges the thoughts and attitudes of the heart. Nothing in all creation is hidden from God's sight. Everything is uncovered and laid bare before the eyes of him to whom we must give account" (NIV).

Dear reader, God knows the things we say, the things we do, the things we think and what is in our heart. Therefore, He is able to guide us with perfect justice.

Now, of course, this is all very threatening to us. We feel threatened by a God who knows everything about us. We try not to think about it. We fear exposure so we try to put God out of our mind. We meditate on how to build a better mousetrap than the living God. Mousetraps aren't threatening, but the living God is a threat to us.

So we wear a mask. We want people to know us but not too well, else they see the real us. Then they may not like us. Because deep down inside, we all know that we're sinners who have rebelled against the sovereign, holy God of the universe. Therefore, we try to hide from God. We try to "cover our trail." Like an ostrich, we put our head in the sand and pretend that God doesn't know.

But we read in Job 11:11, "Surely he recognizes deceitful men; and when he sees evil, does he not take note?" (NIV). Jeremiah wrote of God, " 'Can anyone hide himself in secret places, So I shall not see him' says the LORD" (Jeremiah 23:24 NKJ). Since God is all knowing, He warns us that our sins will find us out, or catch up with us (Numbers 32:23).

But God's all knowledge need not be threatening. Because

even though God knows the worst about us, He still loves us. In Jeremiah, God says, "For I know the thoughts that I think toward you, says the LORD, thoughts of peace and not of evil, to give you a future and a hope. Then you will call upon Me and I will listen to you. And you will seek Me and find Me, when you search for Me with all your heart" (Jeremiah 29:11-13 NKJ).

God has thoughts of peace toward us, not thoughts of evil. We read in 2 Chronicles 16:9, "For the eyes of the LORD run to and fro throughout the whole earth, to show Himself strong on behalf of those whose heart is loyal to Him" (NKJ).

God wants to show Himself strong on our behalf. He desires to use His greatness to bless us. This is why He keeps a close eye on us. David wrote, "As a father pities his children, so the LORD pities those who fear him. For he knows our frame; he remembers that we are dust" (Psalms 103:13-14 RSV). So you see, God deals gently with us. He never gives us more than He knows we can bear.

God knows the trials we go through. In fact, with His perfect knowledge, He allows these trials to come our way when He thinks it is best for us. Job had trials greater than any man. But Job took comfort in God's all-knowledge. He said of God, "But he knows the way that I take; when he has tried me, I shall come forth as gold" (Job 23:10 RSV). God knows when we are falsely accused. Job said to his accusers, "Does he not see my ways, And count all my steps?" (Job 31:4 NKJ).

Finally, King David best summarized God's all knowledge and our response to it with these last words to his son Solomon, "And you, Solomon my son, know the God of your father, and serve him with a whole heart and with a willing mind; for the LORD searches all hearts, and understands every plan and thought. If you seek him, he will be found by you; but if you forsake him, he will cast you off forever" (1 Chronicles 28:9 RSV). *Will you receive this counsel from David as your goal in life?*

Chapter 8—God Is All Knowledge

Review Exercise 7

1. Give your own definition of God's all knowledge.

2. List four ways in which God's all knowledge affects our lives.

   a.

   b.

   c.

   d.

3. How can you apply this information to your life?

9

God Is Everywhere Present

In our last two chapters we've been learning about God's all power and God's all knowledge. God exercises absolute rule over His creation because He is all power. His rule is always consistent with His being because He is all knowledge. Now we are going to see that God can manifest His power anywhere in the universe because He is also everywhere present.

God's Everywhere Presence

God spoke of His everywhere presence with these words from the Prophet Jeremiah, " 'Am I a God near at hand,' says the LORD, 'And not a God afar off? Can anyone hide himself in secret places, So I shall not see him?' says the LORD; 'Do I not fill heaven and earth?' says the LORD" (Jeremiah 23:23-24 NKJ). With this statement, God is revealing the truth that He is everywhere present in His universe. This is why God **knows everything**. God always knows what we are up to, because wherever we go, He's already there.

Now when you and I want to know what's going on in a certain place, we have to go to that place to find out what is happening. And if we want to be somewhere, we have to go to that place to be there in person. You see, "somewhere" is a creature word. We are always "somewhere," while not at the same time, somewhere else.

But God is different. *God is everywhere present in His universe. He never has to go anywhere to find out what is going on because He's there already. He never has to be "somewhere" because He is everywhere.* God fills heaven and earth. This is the truth He is revealing to us through Jeremiah.

God called Jeremiah to warn the Hebrews, that if they didn't turn from their sins, God was going to judge them by allowing Babylon to conquer the land and take them off as slaves. But there were also false prophets in the land. These false prophets tickled the people's ears. They told them just what they wanted to hear. They told them it was all right to practice homosexuality, pornography, adultery, social injustice, worshiping of idols and other sins that grieved God. They even persuaded the religious leaders to be part of the lie. They told the people that, "everything was just fine. Things will continue as they are now. God will surely prosper us because we are the chosen people."

But God said, "Do these false prophets and religious leaders think that I don't know what's going on with them? Do they think I'm limited to one location like the idols they worship? Jeremiah, I want you to remind them that I'm not bound to some geographic location. Jeremiah, tell the people that I'm not 'somewhere,' I'm 'everywhere.' I'm close at hand but I'm also beyond you. I'm near you spiritually, but I'm outside of you geographically. Wherever you are physically, I'm also there. You cannot hide from me because I fill heaven and earth."

God continues to warn Jeremiah, saying, "I hear what

these false teachers are saying. I see how the people are living. And I say things are not going to be all right. I say things are not going to continue as they are now. I say I'm going to judge these people because of their sins." And as we learned in an earlier chapter, God did bring Nebuchadnezzar against Israel and he took the people captive to Babylon.

Dear friend, there is no "secret place" where we can hide from God. Proverbs 15:3 reads, "The eyes of the LORD are in every place, Keeping watch on the evil and the good" (NKJ). We find these words in Psalms 90:8, "You have set our iniquities before You, Our secret sins in the light of your countenance" (NKJ). Job wrote, "Surely he recognizes deceitful men; and when he sees evil, does he not take note?" (Job 11:11 NIV). God sees all sins without searching because He is everywhere.

God's Presence Is Eternal

Since God is eternal, His everywhere presence is eternal. *There never was a time when God wasn't everywhere. There never is a time when He isn't everywhere. And there never will be a time when He won't be everywhere. God has always been everywhere, always is everywhere and always will be everywhere.*

If God was everywhere present in Jeremiah's day, which He was, He is also everywhere present today. *If God saw the sins of the world in Jeremiah's day, which He did, He also sees the sins of our world today.* In fact, out of God's all-knowledge, God would know about the sins of the world today, before "today" ever existed. God has always known what our world would be like today. He even had the Apostle Paul write it down in the Bible. God did this, so that when we who live today see God's word being fulfilled before our very eyes, we would know that the God of the Bible is the one true God who has revealed Himself to us in the person of Jesus Christ.

Let's see what God said about the times we live in today. Paul wrote in 2 Timothy 3:1-5, "But know this, that in the last days perilous times will come: For men will be lovers of themselves, lovers of money, boasters, proud, blasphemers, disobedient to parents, unthankful, unholy, unloving, unforgiving, . . . brutal, despisers of good, traitors, headstrong, haughty, lovers of pleasure rather than lovers of God, having a form of godliness but denying its power. And from such people turn away!" (NKJ).

This certainly describes the present condition of our world, doesn't it? Paul says it is the last days. He describes the last days as perilous times. Because God's everywhere presence is eternal, He sees the sins of the world today just as He did in Jeremiah's day. He knew there would be religious leaders in our day who would tickle people's ears. They would say, "Everything is all right. Things will continue just as they are now. God will surely prosper us because we have 'In God We Trust' written on our coins. We're God's favored nation, so continue in your sins."

But God says something different. *God says He is coming to judge the world.* Listen to these words from the Prophet Zephaniah as he speaks of the days that are just ahead. "The great day of the LORD is near, near and hastening fast; the sound of the day of the LORD is bitter, the mighty man cries aloud there. A day of wrath is that day, a day of distress and anguish, a day of ruin and devastation, a day of darkness and gloom, a day of clouds and thick darkness, a day of trumpet blast and battle cry against the fortified cities and against the lofty battlements. I will bring distress on men, so that they shall walk like the blind, because they have sinned against the LORD; their blood shall be poured out like dust, and their flesh like dung. Neither their silver nor their gold shall be able to deliver them on the day of the wrath of the LORD. In the fire of his jealous wrath, all the earth shall be consumed; for a full, yea, sudden end he will make of all the inhabitants of the earth" (Zephaniah 1:14-18 RSV).

God is everywhere present today. He sees the sins of the nations. And He is moving the world toward that last great battle in preparation for the return of the Lord Jesus Christ to judge the world.

God's Presence Is Infinite

God's everywhere presence is also infinite. Now we creatures are bound by space. We can only be in one place at one time. And to help us cope with our finite condition, we invent all kinds of gadgets such as the telephone, television, radio, etc. Through the telephone we are able to talk to someone who is where we are not. Through the television we are able to see people where we are not. And we have airplanes to speedily carry us somewhere we are not. This all reminds us that we live in time and space. If I'm here, I'm not there. If you are there, you are not here. We're always somewhere at some time.

But God is not bound by space. *Just as God is outside of time, so He is also outside of space.* Both time and space are contained within God. Solomon spoke these words, "But will God indeed dwell on the earth? Behold, the heaven and the highest heavens cannot contain thee; how much less this house which I have built?" (1 Kings 8:27 RSV).

Now let me give you a few illustrations to help explain what I mean when I say that space is contained within God. First, let's consider an ocean. An ocean is full of so many fish that we could never begin to count them. And these fish swim in all parts of the ocean. But wherever they're swimming, they're still in the ocean. The ocean surrounds the fish wherever the fish go. So the ocean is the fishes' environment. They can never get outside of the ocean.

Let's consider the sky. The sky is full of birds. Sometimes they fly north and sometimes they fly south. But wherever they fly, they're still in the sky. The sky is the birds' environment. They can never get outside the sky.

God is like the ocean and the sky, except that He has no bounds. We are like the fish and the birds. *God is our environment.* All of space and all that is within space is contained within God. In Him we live and move and have our being (Acts 17:28).

Now what does this mean to us? It means that we, like the fish and birds, *can never be lost from God's presence.* So if your "flying through the world" has taken you to the ends of the earth, God is there. If your "swimming" has taken you to the blackest, deepest hole in the ocean floor of the world, God is there. (See Psalms 139.) God is with you wherever you go. No matter what challenge lies ahead, what difficult road you must walk on, or what trials you must face, God is there looking out for your good if you know Him in Jesus Christ. Now let's look at some examples from the Bible.

God's Presence With Jacob

Let's begin with Jacob. Jacob, you recall, had stolen his older brother, Esau's, birthright. Jacob wanted the birthright because the blessings of God came with it. Esau actually gave it to Jacob, but later he became angry and wanted to kill Jacob. But Jacob was his mother Rebekah's favorite of the two boys. So Rebekah came up with a plan to save Jacob's life. She tells Isaac her husband that she's concerned that Jacob might marry one of the local pagan girls. And so Isaac, most likely at Rebekah's suggestion, sends Jacob back to the old country to find a wife.

Jacob is going to be exiled from his family. He is going to have to leave all of his friends. He must now leave his familiar surroundings and the comforts of home and make a long, hard dangerous journey. He doesn't know how long he will be gone nor what will happen to him along the way. Although he's going to stay with his uncle Laban he's not even sure if Uncle Laban will even receive him.

So we can see it is a difficult and uncertain time for Jacob. Yet he sets out on his journey leaving all behind. On the way, he stops at a place to rest for the night. The only pillow for his head is an old rock that is laying nearby. As Jacob sleeps, he has a dream. In this dream, Jacob sees a ladder going up to heaven with angels running up and down it. God is at the top of the ladder and He speaks the following words to Jacob, " 'Behold, I am with you and will keep you wherever you go, and will bring you back to this land; for I will not leave you until I have done that which I have spoken to you.' Then Jacob awoke from his sleep and said, 'Surely the LORD is in this place; and I did not know it' "(Genesis 28:15-16 RSV).

What comforting words these were from God. *Jacob thought he was alone, but God was right there with him.* Even though Jacob was in exile without family or friends, God was there. Even though he was making a long, hard dangerous journey, not knowing what was ahead, God was with him. God would keep Jacob in all places. He would never leave Jacob but would be with him wherever he went. Jacob thought he was making the journey by himself. I'm sure he didn't feel like God was anywhere around. But when God spoke, Jacob learned that God was right there with him all the time.

This word from God encouraged Jacob to continue on his journey. Finally he arrived at his uncle's house and worked for him fourteen long years. When the time came for Jacob to make that long return home, God spoke to him again, " 'Return to the land of your fathers and to your kindred, and I will be with you' " (Genesis 31:3 RSV). Again, God promises to be with Jacob.

And, you know, that's just what God says to us today. When we, like Jacob, seek God's blessing through Jesus Christ, the members of our own household, who are like Esau, may hate us. Hear these words from Jesus in Matthew 10, "Do not think that I came to bring peace on earth. I did not come to bring peace but a sword. For I have come 'to set a man against his father, a daughter against her mother, and a daughter-in-law against her mother-in-law.' And a man's foes will be those of his own household" (Matthew 10:34-36 NKJ).

Peter writes, "They think it strange that you do not plunge with them into the same flood of dissipation, and they heap abuse on you" (1 Peter 4:4 NIV).

Dear reader, you may be exiled from your family and friends. Perhaps you have had to leave your familiar surroundings and the comforts of home. Like Jacob, you have set out on a journey with God, leaving all behind. You're going out in new territory. You don't know how long your journey will be nor what lies ahead. *Do not be afraid for God says you are not alone. He is with you. He will keep you in all places. Wherever you go, God is already there waiting to meet your every need.*

Jesus said in Matthew 19:29, "And everyone who has left houses or brothers or sisters or father or mother or wife or children or lands, for My name's sake, shall receive a hundred-fold and inherit everlasting life" (NKJ).

God says in Hebrews 13:5-6, ". . . 'I will never leave you nor forsake you.' So that we may boldly say: 'The Lord is my helper; I will not fear . . .' " (NKJ).

God is with His people every step of their journey. The rock we rest on is Jesus. *Wherever we are in our journey through life, we are always in God's presence.* If your journey takes you to your office at work, God is there. If you are at home washing clothes and changing diapers, God is there. If you are going to school, God is there. If you are on vacation, God is not only traveling with you, but He's also already at your destination. So you don't have to "go somewhere" to be in His presence. Wherever you are you can know, "Surely the Lord is in this place." He will keep you in all places along your journey in this life.

God's Presence With Joshua

God also revealed the truth of His everywhere presence to Joshua. The Hebrews had been wandering around in the wilderness for forty years. Now it is time for them to take their land. God tells Moses that Joshua will be the one who will lead them into the land. So Moses calls the people all together and speaks these words for God, " 'Be strong and of good courage, do not fear or be in dread of them: for it is the LORD your God who goes with you; he will not fail you nor forsake you.' Then Moses summoned Joshua, and said to him in sight of all Israel, 'Be strong and of good courage; for you shall go with this people into the land which the LORD has sworn to their fathers to give them; and you shall put them in possession of it. It is the LORD who goes before you; he will be with you, he will not fail you or forsake you; do not fear or be dismayed' " (Deuteronomy 31:6-8 RSV).

Then when the actual time came for the Hebrews to take the land, God spoke once again to Joshua, "Have I not commanded you? Be strong and of good courage; be not frightened, neither be dismayed; for the LORD your God is with you wherever you go" (Joshua 1:9 RSV).

This is God's word of comfort to all of us who know Him through Christ Jesus. Jesus is the one greater than Joshua who will lead us into God's rest. He is the captain of our salvation who has gone before us and destroyed all our enemies. *Be strong and of good courage. Do not be afraid, for the Lord God goes with you. He will not fail you nor forsake you.* He is a God who is far off but desires to come near you through the Lord Jesus Christ. Because of this wonderful revelation of God's everywhere presence, Jesus said, "Go therefore and make disciples of all nations, baptizing them in the name of the Father and of the Son and of the Holy Spirit, teaching them to observe all things that I have commanded you; and lo, I am with you always, even to the end of the age" (Matthew 28:19-20 NKJ).

Chapter 9—God Is Everywhere Present

Review Exercise 8

1. Give your own definition of God's everywhere presence.

2. Explain how it is possible for God to be everywhere present.

3. Write out the following Scripture passages:

   a. Hebrews 13:5-6—

   b. Matthew 28:18-20—

4. How can you apply this knowledge to your life?

10

God Is Unchanging

In this final chapter on God's majestic attributes, we are going to learn something wonderful about God. We're going to learn that God is unchanging. We'll also discover three areas in which God never changes and how this fantastic truth about God applies to our lives today.

God Never Changes

First of all, God Himself never changes. We read in Malachi 3:6, "For I am the LORD, I do not change . . ."(NKJ). God says He does not change. James was referring to God's unchanging nature when he wrote, "Every good gift and every perfect gift is from above, and comes down from the Father of lights, with whom there is no variation or shadow of turning" (James 1:17 NKJ).

All that God has made changes. We use the word "mutable" to speak of anything that has capability of change. When there is a drastic change, we call it a mutation. Anything that does not change we say is "immutable." Only God is immutable. *Only God never changes.* But all that God has created is mutable.

God's created universe is always changing. This is what James is referring to in the passage we've just read. The lights that God placed in the heavens are always changing. For example, the sun, which is a star, is constantly losing its ability to give light. Of course we don't realize this because it is happening gradually over the course of time. The light which the moon reflects from the sun also changes. Sometimes it is a full moon, while at other times it is a half-moon, quarter moon, etc. If there is an eclipse, there's little or no light at all. The weather is always changing so we pay people to forecast what they think it might be. The earth is also drastically changing.

King David compared the immutability of God with the mutability of the universe with these words, "Of old You laid the foundation of the earth, And the heavens are the work of Your hands. They will perish, but You will endure; Yes, all of them will grow old like a garment; Like a cloak You will change them, And they will be changed. But You are the same, And Your years will have no end" (Psalms 102:25-27 NKJ). (See also Hebrews 1:10-13.) David compared the world to an old garment that was worn with use and would eventually be discarded. But he said, "God, You are the same!"

We creatures are always changing. We are today what we were not yesterday; we'll be tomorrow what we are not today. One day we have a lot of hair and then all of a sudden it's gone. Our waistline is always changing. Sometimes we can get into our clothes and sometimes we can't. Our physical well-being is always changing. Some days we feel good and some days we feel bad. And we're always changing our minds. One day we think we're going to do something and then the next day we decide to do something differently. Our friends change, our attitudes change and our disposition changes.

The only thing that's constant about creatures is change. And this constant change always keeps us a little off balance, bewildered, confused and uncertain. So we're never sure about where to go, what to do or whom to trust. Life is sort of unsettling, isn't it? But I've got some great news for us! *We human creatures, who are always changing, can find rest in a God who never changes.*

God's Immutable Nature Is Eternal

Since God is eternal, His immutable (unchanging) nature is eternal. This means that *God in His being, never has changed, is not now changing and never will change. He always was, always is and always will be the same in His being. What God was yesterday, He is today, and what He is today, He will be tomorrow.* God never differs from Himself.

Let me explain it to you this way. God was sovereign, is sovereign and will be sovereign. God was all-power, is all-power and will be all-power. God was all-knowing, is all-knowing, and will be all-knowing. God was everywhere present, is everywhere present and will be everywhere present. God was holy, love, just, good, is holy, love, just, good and will be holy, love, just and good. God is the same yesterday, today and forever.

Now there are a lot of people who believe that God changed from the Old Testament to the New Testament. They think the God of the Old Testament is a God of wrath, while the God of the New Testament is a God of love. In their minds, God changed somewhere between the two testaments.

Some people even think that there are two different Gods, one in the Old Testament and another in the New Testament. Maybe you have thought this way. If you have had this concern, let me encourage you to read the Bible a little more closely. *Because God presents Himself in both testaments as the one true God who changes not.* For example, in the Old Testament, God reveals His love just as clearly as He does His wrath. Every Jew who is alive today is a living testimony to the love of God. Likewise, in the New Testament, Jesus speaks more of hell than He does heaven. God is eternal and therefore unchanging in His being. *The God who changes not is our link to the people in the Bible.*

Now we have a difficult time understanding the Bible because the setting of the Bible is in a different time and culture than ours. It is hard for a modern, freeway-driving, technologically-oriented city slicker to understand a story written in a semi-oriental, agricultural setting. So we get confused and think that much of the Bible has no meaning for us today. Our problem is that, although we're looking in the right place, we're looking at the wrong thing.

Now here is something very important to remember. *When you study the Bible, focus your attention on the God of the Bible rather than the people in the Bible.* We have a hard time identifying with the people because our world is so different from their world. But God gave us the Bible, not so much to learn about people, but primarily to learn about Him. And God never changes.

If we want to know God's attitude about life today, we see what His attitude was about life then. If we want to know what to expect from God today, we see how He acted towards His creatures then. The mind, heart and actions of God in today's world are the same as they were in the world of the Bible. The penalty for sin is still death, and the gift of God is still eternal life through Jesus Christ our Lord.

God's Immutable Nature Is Infinite

God is not only unchanging, He is also *unchangeable.* God is unchangeable because His immutable being is infinite. Remember that infinite means limitless, boundless and measureless. When God reveals Himself as the immutable, infinite One, that means He never changes, never! Someone who never ever changes is unchangeable.

Because God is perfection without limits, He doesn't have to change. He can't change for the better for that would mean that He is not perfect. Being perfect, He certainly can't change for the worse. We read in Numbers 23:19, "God is not a man, that He should lie, Nor a son of man, that He should repent. Has He said, and will He not do it? Or has He spoken, and will He not make it good?" (NKJ) Samuel said to King Saul, "And also the Strength of Israel will not lie nor relent. For He is not a man, that He should relent" (1 Samuel 15:29 NKJ).

Now what does this mean to us today? It means that in all of our dealings with God, we are the ones who must change. Therefore, in our prayers, it does us no good to try to twist God's arm to do us a little favor if that favor would require God to act out of His character. He simply cannot do it. So don't waste your breath with selfish prayers and petitions that would require God to act incompatibly with Himself and violate His character.

In the New Testament, Jesus said we could have anything we ask from the Father in His name (John 14:13-14). In Bible times, to do something in someone's name was to do it in their character. So to ask God for something in Jesus' name is to ask in His character. And to ask in Jesus' character requires us to live in His character. Unfortunately, most of the prayers we ask are really in our own name. We just put Jesus' name on the end of it, thinking that this makes our prayer "kosher." But it doesn't.

God will not answer "yes" to our selfish prayers nor bend His will to ours. We must bend our will to His. We must change and make our desires to be one with God. When God's desires become our desires, then God will give us the desires of our heart. We learn this from Psalms 37:4-5 which reads, "Delight yourself also in the LORD, And He shall give you the desires of your heart. Commit your way to the LORD, trust also in Him, and He shall bring it to pass" (NKJ).

On several occasions, however, the Bible says that God repented. This seems to be in conflict with what we have just learned. But as we examine the situation closer, we find that in each case, it was actually the people who changed not God.

Genesis 6:6 says, "And the LORD was sorry that He had made man on the earth, and He was grieved in His heart" (NKJ). To understand this verse, we must realize why God made man. We've already learned why God made man. God made man to share in His glory. This was and still is God's desire for His creatures. But because God is holy, He cannot share His glory with an unrepentant sinner. So if the sinner doesn't change, his destiny will change from that which God intended for him.

We read in Genesis 6:5, "Then the LORD saw that the wickedness of man was great in the earth, and that every intent of the thoughts of his heart was only evil continually" (NKJ). Well, God can't share His glory with this kind of creature. In view of this, their destiny changed from one of glory to one of destruction. God destroyed them all with a flood, except for Noah who was a just man in God's sight.

We see this same situation with Jonah. God told Jonah to go to Nineveh and tell the people that God was going to destroy the city in forty days because of their wickedness. When the people heard Jonah's message they believed him, repented and asked God to spare them. The King of Nineveh said, "But let man and beast be covered with sackcloth, and cry mightily to God; yes, let every one turn from his evil way and from the violence that is in his hands. Who can tell if God will turn and relent, and turn away from His fierce anger, so that we may not perish?" (Jonah 3:8-9 NKJ).

Then we read, "Then God saw their works, that they turned from their evil way; and God relented from the disaster that He had said He would bring upon them, and He did not do it" (Jonah 3:10 NKJ).

So we see that God did not change. The Ninevites changed. Therefore, their destiny changed because God could now deal with them differently than He originally said. Later they fell back into their wickedness and God did destroy them. (See Nahum 1—3.)

God's Decree Never Changes

The second area in which God never changes is His *decree*. God's decree or purpose is sometimes called His counsel. Isaiah 14:24 reads, "The LORD of hosts has sworn: 'As I have planned, so shall it be, and as I have purposed, so shall it stand . . .' " (RSV). And in a verse we looked at earlier, Isaiah says, "Remember the former things of old, For I am God, and there is no other; I am God, and there is none like Me, Declaring the end from the beginning, And from ancient times things that are not yet done, Saying, 'My counsel shall stand, And I will do all My pleasure' " (Isaiah 46:9-10 NKJ).

Man, in his pride, thinks that he is ruling over this world and that God is adjusting His plans and purposes to keep up with man. But God tells a different story. We read in Psalms 33:10-12, "The LORD brings the counsel of the nations to nothing; He makes the plans of the peoples of no effect. The counsel of the LORD stands forever . . ." (NKJ). Proverbs 19:21 says, "There are many plans in a man's heart, Nevertheless the LORD'S counsel—that will stand" (NKJ).

And what is the decree or counsel of the Lord? We've learned about it in an earlier chapter. *The decree or counsel of the Lord is to glorify Himself through the Lord Jesus Christ and share this glory with all who will come to Christ* (Ephesians 3:11).

In John 17, Jesus, knowing that His time of death was near, lifted up His eyes to heaven and prayed, ". . . Father, the hour has come. Glorify Your Son, that Your Son also may glorify You, as you have given Him authority over all flesh, that He should give eternal life to as many as You have given Him. And this is eternal life, that they may know You, the only true God, and Jesus Christ whom you have sent. I have glorified You on the earth. I have finished the work which you have given Me to do. And now, O Father, glorify Me together with Yourself, with the glory which I had with You before the world was" (John 17:1-5 NKJ).

Further on in that same chapter, Jesus prayed for those who would receive Him. As He looked to the cross, He said, "I pray for them. I do not pray for the world but for those whom You have given Me, for they are Yours. And all Mine are Yours, and Yours are Mine, and I am glorified in them. Now I am no longer in the world, but these are in the world, and I come to You. Holy Father, keep through Your name those whom You have given Me, that they may be one as We are" (John 17:9-11 NKJ).

Jesus continues in John 17:20-24, "I do not pray for these alone [His immediate disciples], but also for those who will believe in Me through their word; that they all may be one, as You, Father, are in Me, and I in You; that they also may be one in Us, that the world may believe that You sent Me. And the glory which You gave Me I have given them, that they may be one just as We are one: I in them, and You in Me; that they may be made perfect in one, and that the world may know that You have sent Me, and have loved them as You have loved Me. Father, I desire that they also whom you have given Me may be with Me where I am, that they may behold My glory which You have given Me; for You loved Me before the foundation of the world" (NKJ).

This is God's unchanging, unchangeable decree. And to those who have come to Jesus, Paul writes, "And I am sure that he who began a good work in you will bring it to completion at the day of Jesus Christ" (Philippians 1:6 RSV).

Let's see another statement about God's eternal decree from the Letter to the Hebrews. It reads, "For when God made a promise to Abraham, because He could swear to no one greater, He swore by himself, saying, 'Surely blessing I will bless you, and multiplying I will multiply you.' And so, after he had patiently endured, he obtained the promise. For men indeed swear by the greater, and an oath for confirmation is for them an end of all dispute. Thus God, determining to show more abundantly to the heirs of promise the immutability of His counsel, confirmed it by an oath, that by two immutable things in which it is impossible for God to lie, we might have strong consolation, who have fled for refuge to lay hold of the hope set before us. This hope we have as an anchor of the soul, both sure and steadfast . . .' " (Hebrews 6:13-19 NKJ).

This passage of Scripture speaks of the covenant God made with Abraham and all who would come into the covenant through Jesus Christ. God promised Abraham that He would bless him. And to encourage Abraham to rest in God's promise, God even went a step further. **God not** only gave His Word, which would certainly be enough, but He also swore by Himself to do it. God entered into an oath with Himself. He confirmed the immutability of His counsel by swearing to fulfill His Word. *So we have God's promise and God's oath that He will raise us up at the last day and glorify us with Jesus Christ. This is the hope set before us. This is the anchor of our soul.*

But those who do not know God through Jesus Christ have no such anchor. When the storms come their way, they are tossed to and fro in the sea of life. Jude said that the wicked are like clouds without water carried along by the winds, fruitless trees uprooted, raging waves of the sea casting up the foam of their own shame, wandering stars to whom is reserved the blackness of darkness forever (Jude 12-13).

Isaiah wrote, "But the wicked are like the troubled sea, When it cannot rest, Whose waters cast up mire and dirt. 'There is no peace,' says God, 'for the wicked' " (Isaiah 57:20-21 NKJ).

In contrast, we who know Jesus have peace. We are anchored in Him who gives us a calm assurance that He is ours and we are His. *This hope within us gives permanance and stability to the Christian in the midst of the stormy seas of life.* We have a hope that ends all strife. It is the Word of the unchanging, unchangeable God. Faithful is He who called you who also will do it (1 Thessalonians 5:24).

God's Word Never Changes

Finally, *God's Word never changes.* In Psalms 119:89 we learn, "Forever, O LORD, Your word is settled in heaven" (NKJ). Isaiah wrote, "The grass withers, the flowers fades; but the word of our God will stand forever" (Isaiah 40:8 RSV). (See also 1 Peter 1:24-25.) Jesus said in Matthew 24:35, "Heaven and earth will pass away, but My words will by no means pass away" (NKJ). Paul wrote to Titus that God, who cannot lie, promised us eternal life before the world began (Titus 1:2).

In reference to the immutable counsel of God, Jesus said, "Let not your heart be troubled; You believe in God, believe also in Me. In My Father's house are many mansions; if it were not so, I would have told you. I go to prepare a place for you. And if I go and prepare a place for you, I will come again and receive you to Myself; that where I am, there you may be also" (John 14:1-3, NKJ).

Finally, we read in Hebrews 13:8, "Jesus Christ is the same yesterday and today and forever" (NIV). *The unchanging, unchangeable God has revealed Himself to us through the Lord Jesus Christ that in Him we might have life.*

This concludes our discussion of God's majestic attributes. I hope that these chapters have helped raise your consciousness of the greatness of God. He is a God worthy to be worshiped, trusted and obeyed. Do you really worship Him? Have you trusted Him? Are you now obeying Him? I pray that you are and that glorifying God through worship, trust and obedience will become the center of your life and your reason for living. To God be the glory both now and forever.

Chapter 10—God Is Unchanging

Review Exercise 9

1. What do we mean when we say that God never changes?

2. List three areas in which God never changes and explain how He is the same in each area.

   a.

   b.

   c.

3. How can you apply this knowledge to your life?

PART 3

GOD'S MORAL ATTRIBUTES

11
God Is Holy

Whereas God's majestic attributes speak of His greatness, God's moral attributes reveal His character. As mentioned in the introductory chapter, God, in His character, is perfectly holy, perfectly loving, perfectly just and perfectly good. In this chapter, we're going to learn about God's perfect holiness.

Throughout the Bible, God is considered to be great and awesome because of His holiness. So we need to begin this chapter with an understanding of the biblical meaning of the word "holy." *In the Bible, the word holy means separate or set apart.* It is not only applied to God, but it is also applied to anything that God sets apart for Himself. Whatever God sets apart for Himself is considered to be holy by the very act of God setting that object apart. But only God is naturally holy. Only God is set apart by His very nature. We learn this in Revelation 15:4 which reads, "Who shall not fear You,

O Lord, and glorify Your name? For You alone are holy . . ." (NKJ).

God Is Glorious in His Holiness

The Hebrews worshiped God for His holiness. We all know the story of how God delivered them from Egypt. As soon as they were safe on the other side of the Red Sea, they began to sing a song of praise to God. They sang, "Who is like You, O LORD, among the gods? Who is like You, glorious in holiness, Fearful in praises, doing wonders?" (Exodus 15:11 NKJ).

The Hebrews were not asking a question but were expressing a truth which they had learned about God. The truth which they had learned was that "there is none like God." *To the Hebrews, it was God's holiness that impressed them more than anything else.*

Now you would think that God's power would be foremost on their mind. Because it was God's power that just delivered them from Egypt. *But it was God's holiness that distinguished Him. It was God's holiness that so completely overwhelmed the Hebrews that they worshiped Him with a profound, reverential respect.* Later, a woman named Hannah sang, "There is none holy like the LORD . . ." (1 Samuel 2:2 NKJ). To help us understand what the Hebrews were singing about, we now want to learn about some specific areas of God's holiness.

God's Works and Ways Are Holy

First, God's works and ways are holy. It should be obvious that everything God does is holy because God is holy. Psalms 145:17 tells us, "The LORD is righteous in all His ways, Gracious [holy] in all His works" (NKJ). This just means that God does things differently from the way we do them. God spoke of His holiness through Isaiah with these words, " 'For My thoughts are not your thoughts, Nor are your ways My ways,' says the LORD. 'For as the heavens are higher than the earth, So are My ways higher than your ways, And my thoughts than your thoughts' " (Isaiah 55:8-9 NKJ).

122

So you see, God doesn't think the way we think. He doesn't act the way we act. He doesn't do things the way we do them. If you want to know what God would do in a given situation, meditate on His Word with a teachable, humble spirit and He will show you.

God's Character Is Holy

God is also separate from His creatures in His *moral character*. God is morally perfect and pure so that He is without sin. Habakkuk 1:13 says that God is so holy, so separate, so morally pure, that He cannot even look upon sin, much less be around it. We learn from Psalms 5:4, "For You are not a God who takes pleasure in wickedness, nor shall evil dwell with You" (NKJ). Isaiah writes, "Behold, the LORD'S hand is not shortened, That it cannot save; Nor His ear heavy, That it cannot hear. But your iniquities have separated you from your God; And your sins have hidden His face from you, So that He will not hear" (Isaiah 59:1-2 NKJ). Later in the New Testament, Paul wrote, "for all have sinned and fall short of the glory [holiness] of God" (Romans 3:23 NKJ).

So when the Bible says that God is holy, it means He is separate and different from all that He has created. God is not like any of His creatures. There is an infinite gap separating the Creator from His creation. The main problem with the Hebrews (and us) is that they kept forgetting that God was holy. God was always having to remind them. On one occasion He said, "These things you have done and I have been silent; you thought that I was one like yourself. But now I rebuke you, and lay the charge before you" (Psalms 50:21 RSV). As a reminder, the Hebrews made up songs about God's holiness. King David wrote one which says, "Sing praise to the LORD, you saints of His, And give thanks at the remembrance of His holy name" (Psalms 30:4 NKJ).

Holy Encounters

The people in the Bible soon learned that an encounter with the holy God was a frightening experience which they would not soon forget. You recall, when Moses approached God in the burning bush, God said, " '. . . Do not come near; put off your shoes from your feet, for the place on which you are standing is holy ground' " (Exodus 3:5 RSV). Well, after this divine pronouncement, Moses hid his face and was afraid to look at God.

Isaiah also had such an encounter with God. He gives the following account, "In the year that King Uzziah died I saw the Lord sitting upon a throne, high and lifted up; and his train filled the temple. Above him stood the seraphim; each had six wings: with two he covered his face, and with two he covered his feet, and with two he flew. And one called to another and said: 'Holy, holy, holy is the LORD of hosts; the whole earth is full of his glory.' And the foundations of the thresholds shook at the voice of him who called, and the house was filled with smoke. And I said: 'Woe is me! For I am lost; for I am a man of unclean lips, and I dwell in the midst of a people of unclean lips; for my eyes have seen the King, the LORD of hosts!' " (Isaiah 6:1-5 RSV).

The Prophet Habakkuk had an encounter with God's holiness that devastated him. After God spoke to him, Habakkuk said, "I heard and my heart pounded, my lips quivered at the sound; decay crept into my bones, and my legs trembled" (Habakkuk 3:16 NIV).

And after God got through with Job, the only thing Job could say was, " 'I had heard of thee by the hearing of the ear, but now my eye sees thee; therefore I despise myself, and repent in dust and ashes' " (Job 42:5-6 RSV).

Every time someone in the Bible had an encounter with God, they were reduced to nothing. His holiness terrified them. His glory overwhelmed them. There was no pride, no ego, no arrogance and no self-exaltation left in one who had encountered the holy God.

God's People Are Holy

But God has a problem. *How can He reveal His holiness to weak, fragile man without completely destroying man by the awesomeness of that very holiness He wants to reveal?*

There's only one way. God says, *"Give me a company of people, a people who will be my people, and I will reveal my holiness through them."* God then chose Abraham and his descendants as a nation of people through which He would reveal His holiness. And God entered into covenant with them. And just as soon as God brought the Hebrews out of Egypt He let them in on His plan. He said, "Now therefore, if you will obey my voice and keep my covenant, you shall be my own possession among all peoples; for all the earth is mine, and you shall be to me a kingdom of priests and a holy nation" (Exodus 19:5-6 RSV).

God chose the Hebrews to be a holy nation. They were a nation set apart and different from the ungodly nations around them. They were to be God's own people. They were to be as lights shining forth the glory of God in a world of darkness. *God's separateness was to be seen in the separateness of His people. The world would see God's holiness in His people and, as a result, they would bow before Him.*

To let His people know just how separate He was, God came down to them on the top of a mountain. It was an impressive appearance the Hebrews would never forget. God said to Moses, "Put limits for the people around the mountain and tell them, 'Be careful that you do not go up the mountain or touch the foot of it. Whoever touches the mountain shall surely be put to death. He shall surely be stoned or shot with arrows; not a hand is to be laid on him. Whether man or animal, he shall not be permitted to live.' Only when the ram's horn sounds a long blast may they go up to the mountain" (Exodus 19:12-13 NIV).

The people did as they were told. When God appeared, there was a terrific thunder and lightning storm, and a huge cloud came down upon the mountain. This was followed by a long blast as from a ram's horn. When the people heard the blast, they all trembled. All of the mountain was covered with smoke as God descended upon it in the form of fire. Smoke billowed into the sky as from a furnace, and the whole mountain shook with a violent earthquake. It was an awesome sight. The people stood at a distance shaking with fear. When they could no longer stand it, they said to Moses, ". . . Speak to us yourself and we will listen. But do not have God speak to us or we will die" (Exodus 20:19 NIV).

Then God gave them the Ten Commandments. He also gave them civil laws to live by as a nation and laws for personal conduct. Along with these laws, God also gave Moses instructions for building a Tabernacle. There were two rooms inside the Tabernacle. The outer room was called the holy place. Only the priests could go into the holy place. It was hid from the view of the people by a curtain which kept the common Hebrew from entering the room. The other inner room was called the holy of holies. This was the most separate room because it was in this room that God dwelled in the midst of His people.

A thick veil separated the holy of holies from the outer room. Only the high priest could go into the holy of holies. Yet, he could only go in one day a year. And on that special day, he had incense billowing up in front of him to protect him from the awesome presence of God. Through all of these physical means, God was showing His people that He was a holy God and that you didn't just casually come into His presence.

Then God began to explain to the Hebrews their responsibility as His covenant people. He said to Moses, "Say to all the congregation of the people of Israel, You shall be holy; for I the LORD your God am holy" (Leviticus 19:2 RSV). *So God instructed the Hebrews to be separate from their pagan neighbors. The world would see God's holiness in His people. Then they would turn from their evil ways and worship the one true God.*

The Mystery of Mysteries

But the mystery of all mysteries is how can a holy God dwell in the midst of a sinful people. We find the answer to this mystery in Isaiah 57:15, "For thus says the High and Lofty One Who inhabits eternity, whose name is Holy, 'I dwell in the high and holy place, With him who has a contrite and humble spirit, To revive the spirit of the

126

humble, and to revive the heart of the contrite ones' "(NKJ). God also spoke these words through Isaiah, "But on this one will I look: On him who is poor and of a contrite spirit, and who trembles at My word" (Isaiah 66:2 NKJ). David wrote in Psalms 24:3-5, "Who may ascend into the hill of the LORD? Or who may stand in His holy place? He who has clean hands and a pure heart . . . He shall receive blessing from the LORD, And righteousness from the God of his salvation" (NKJ).

God says He will dwell in the midst of a people who would humble themselves before Him. But the Hebrews seldom did this from their heart. They thought that God's holiness stopped with outward acts. So they tried to approach God based on outward acts of holiness rather than an inward holiness of the heart. They began to add rule upon rule and regulation upon regulation to the basic laws God had given them. In other words, they missed the whole idea that God was desiring a holiness of the heart that would produce outward acts of holiness. God said, "There is only one thing left to do to get them to understand. I'm going to have to clothe my holiness with flesh and blood so that my people will understand. I'll become one of them and walk among them as a living example for them to see."

Jesus the Holy One

God began to raise up prophets to tell of His coming. When the time finally came, God sent an angel to Mary. Luke tells us what the angel said to Mary, ". . . The Holy Spirit will come upon you, and the power of the Highest will overshadow you; therefore, also, that Holy One who is to be born will be called the Son of God" (Luke 1:35 NKJ). That holy child born to Mary was Jesus of Nazareth. Jesus was different from all other humans. He was born of a virgin. Demons recognized Him as the "holy one of God" (Luke 4:35, Mark 1:24). John the Baptist said of Jesus, "I'm not worthy to unloose his sandals, but when I'm around Him, I take mine off" (Matthew 3:11, paraphrased). On one occasion, Jesus revealed just a glimpse of His glory to His disciples who, upon seeing it, fell on their faces and were filled with awe (Matthew 17:7).

At the age of thirty, Jesus began to preach the real meaning of God's holiness. He said, "Blessed are the poor in spirit, For theirs is the kingdom of heaven. Blessed are those who mourn, For they shall be comforted. Blessed are the meek, For they shall inherit the earth. Blessed are those who hunger and thirst for righteousness, For they shall be filled. Blessed are the merciful, For they shall obtain mercy. Blessed are the pure in heart, For they shall see God. Blessed are the peacemakers, For they shall be called sons of God. Blessed are those who are persecuted for righteousness' sake, For theirs is the kingdom of heaven. Blessed are you when they revile and persecute you, and say all kinds of evil against you falsely for My sake. Rejoice and be exceedingly glad, for great is your reward in heaven, for so they persecuted the prophets who were before you . . . . For I say to you, that unless your righteousness exceeds the righteousness of the scribes and Pharisees, you will by no means enter the kingdom of heaven" (Matthew 5:3-12, 20 NKJ).

Here was the heart of God's holiness, a way of life completely different from the world's standards. *But how can sinful man live up to these standards?* We can't. This is why we must humble ourselves before God. This is why we must receive Jesus as the holy One Himself who died for our sins. We can draw near to God through Jesus Christ who was holiness in the flesh.

People often ask, "But how does this happen?" *It happens in this way.* When we invite Christ into our life, He sends us the Holy Spirit. The Holy Spirit is God Himself coming to live in our hearts. So that through the Holy Spirit, God actually writes His laws on the fleshly tablets of our hearts. He will cause us to walk in His ways and keep His commandments. He will be our God and we will be His people (Jeremiah 31:31).

God's Holiness in Us

And what is God's desire for those who know Him by

Jesus Christ? Peter tells us with these words, "But you are a chosen generation, a royal priesthood, a holy nation, His own special people, that you may proclaim the praises of Him who called you out of darkness into His marvelous light" (1 Peter 2:9 NKJ).

God has chosen us to be a holy people, a people set apart and different from those around us who do not know Jesus Christ as the Holy One of God. We are to be in the world but not of this world. We are now God's people. We are a separate people because we have received the "separate Spirit." We are to let His light shine through us and live as the salt of the earth (Matthew 5:13-16). When we live in this way, God's holiness will be seen in us. God will be glorified in His people.

Peter further wrote, "Beloved, I beg you as sojourners and pilgrims, abstain from fleshly lusts which war against the soul, having your conduct honorable among the Gentiles, that when they speak against you as evildoers, they may, by your good works which they observe, glorify God in the day of visitation" (1 Peter 2:11-12 NKJ).

Once more we read from Peter, "Therefore gird up the loins of your mind, be sober, and rest your hope fully upon the grace that is to be brought to you at the revelation of Jesus Christ; as obedient children, not conforming yourselves to the former lusts as in your ignorance; but as He who has called you is holy, you also be holy in all your conduct, because it is written, 'Be holy, for I am holy' " (1 Peter 1:13-16 NKJ).

The Greek word that is translated "holy" is also translated "saint." According to the Bible, a saint is someone whom God has set apart for Himself. The very act of God setting you apart makes you a saint. (See 1 Corinthians 1:2.) You may not feel like a saint, and you may not always act like a saint, but God says that you are because He has set you apart from the world unto Himself by Jesus Christ.

Paul wrote these words to the Romans, "I beseech you therefore, brethren, by the mercies of God, that you present your bodies a living sacrifice, holy, acceptable to God, which

129

is your reasonable service. And do not be conformed to this world, but be transformed by the renewing of your mind, that you may prove what is that good and acceptable and perfect will of God" (Romans 12:1-2 NKJ). (See also 2 Corinthians 6:14—17:1.)

The question that many Christians ask is, "How do I act like a saint? How do I live this separated life?" To answer this question, we must first say how we do not live this separated life. It is not by trying to keep a list of rules and regulations and do's and don'ts. It is not by legalistic codes designed to control our behavior. *But it is by allowing the Holy Spirit to live this separated life through us.* He is the only One who can do it.

Are you living this separated life? When you completely surrender to the Lordship of Jesus Christ in every area of your life, the Holy Spirit moves into that area and lives that separate life as only He can live it. He begins to change you on the inside. His desires become your desires. His ways become your ways. His character becomes your character. This is what Paul meant when he wrote the Philippians, "for it is God who works in you both to will and to do for his good pleasure" (Philippians 2:13 NKJ). *When the world sees this outworking of God's holiness in you, they will begin to understand that He is different, and that they too must turn from their sinful ways to serve the living God, who, by nature, is holy.*

Review Exercise 10

1. Define the biblical meaning of the word "holy."

2. How does a Christian live a holy life?

3. How can you apply this knowledge to your life?

12
God Is Love

Perhaps the greatest revelation God has given us about himself is that He is love. We read in 1 John 4:7-8, "Beloved, let us love one another, for love is of God; and everyone who loves is born of God and knows God. He who does not love does not know God, for God is love" (NKJ). *Like all of God's attributes, love is not just something God does and has; love is who God is in His very being.* God cannot help but love because He is love. All expressions of love originate from the One Himself whose very nature is love. You see, when God created us in His image, He filled us with His love. That original image of His love has been tainted by sin, so that what is left is just a dim reflection of what was in the beginning. But even this imperfect love which remains has God as its source. For love is of God.

Yet, when man rebelled against God, his understanding of God became perverted. His mind became so darkened that he lost knowledge of **God's** love. But, still finding he needed God, man began to make many false gods to worship. However, in his guilt and sin, man could only envision harsh, cruel, angry gods whose demands were void of love. Many people today still have this concept of God. *Yet God desires to reveal and restore His own perfect love within each of his fallen creatures.* It is only through God's love that we can truly experience fellowship with Him and each other because God is love.

Understanding God's Love

But we must understand God's love in light of all that God is in His total self. For God is more than just love. You see, *God does not consist of different component parts which He sometimes uses and sometimes puts on the shelf.* God does not have a part of Himself which is holy, another part which is love, another part which is just and another part which is good. God is all of this all the time. He is within Himself a unity having perfect harmony within Himself. This means that God cannot exercise any one of His attributes at the expense of any other of His attributes. All that God is functions together in perfect harmony with Himself, always. So God always acts in harmony with Himself.

When God loves, His love is consistent with His being. His love flows simultaneously and in perfect harmony with His holiness, justice and goodness. And we can get into serious trouble when we focus in on any one of God's moral attributes to the degree that we overlook, ignore or exclude the entirety of God. *So we need to understand God's love within the context of His whole being.* Otherwise, God becomes nothing more to us than a cosmic Santa Claus. In order to help us have a balanced understanding of God, we are now going to consider four aspects of His love.

God's Love Is Holy

First of all, God's love is *holy*. We learned in the previous chapter that the word holy means separate. God's love is separate or different from human love. Human love is regulated by passion and emotion. It is basically sentimental by nature. Contrary to human love, God's love is regulated by who He is, not by outside factors.

Since God is holy, His love is holy. It's a different kind of love. It's a love that loves the sinner but hates sin. We learn from 1 John 1:5, "This is the message which we have heard from Him and declare to you, that God is light and in Him is no darkness at all" (NKJ). In the Bible, the word light is often used to speak of life and moral purity, whereas darkness often refers to death and sin. God is separated from His creatures in His moral being. He is perfectly pure and cannot dwell where there is sin.

God says to His creatures, "The day you sin you shall surely die" (see Genesis 2:17). Death means separation from God. This must be, because God's love is a holy love. It is not a good-natured sentimentalism that is indifferent to sin. Unlike us, God doesn't "wink" at sin. God's holiness banished Adam and Eve from the garden, but God's love covered them with the skins of an animal. Then God Himself promised that one day He would come to the earth and take away their sins (Genesis 3:15).

So God's holiness says, "The penalty for sin is death." God's justice says, "The penalty must be paid." God's goodness says, "But I don't want them to pay it." Finally, God's love says, "I'll come to earth and pay it for them." God's holiness and God's love meet at the cross of Jesus Christ. God in His perfect holiness will not excuse sin. But in His perfect love, God will pardon the sinner who accepts Jesus Christ as the One who died in the sinner's place.

The same Jesus that said, "Father, forgive them, for they do not know what they do" (Luke 23:34) also said, "Fear God who has the power to kill and cast into hell" (Matthew 10:28). Jesus was reminding us that we should have reverence for the holiness of God's love. For God must deal with sin by eternally separating Himself from those who continue in their evil ways.

For those who know God, He will allow difficult trials to come into their life if He knows these trials will produce holiness in us. His holiness won't shield us from trials, but His love will never allow us a trial too difficult for us to handle. His grace is sufficient for all our needs, and in our weakness His strength is made perfect.

God will not give us happiness without first giving us holiness. In fact, a Christian cannot be happy until he is holy. Any Christian who is out of fellowship with God can testify that he is the most unhappy person he knows. So God says to us, "My son, do not despise the chastening of the LORD, Nor detest His correction; for whom the LORD loves He corrects, Just as a father the son in whom he delights" (Proverbs 3:11-12 NKJ). The writer of Hebrews says that this chastening is that we might be partakers of God's holiness (Hebrews 12:10).

God knows that His children are a lot like teabags; we aren't worth much until we've been through some hot water. And, when necessary, God, in His holiness, puts us through some of this hot water. But His love says, "When you pass through the waters, I will be with you; And through the rivers, they shall not overflow you. When you walk through the fire, you shall not be burned, Nor shall the flame scorch you" (Isaiah 43:2 NKJ).

God's Love Is Eternal

God's love is also *eternal.* God's love is eternal because He is eternal. It's so tragic that many people don't understand this. When they read the Old Testament all they can see is a God of wrath. They miss His love. They think that God changed somewhere between the two testaments, or worse, that there are two different Gods, one in the Old Testament and one in the New Testament. But, of course, this is impossible because God is the eternal One who is always the same and changes not.

We read in Jeremiah 31:3, "The LORD appeared to us in the past, saying, 'I have loved you with an everlasting love; I have drawn you with loving-kindness' (NIV). Jeremiah also wrote, "The steadfast love of the LORD never ceases, his mercies never come to an end; they are new every morning;

great is thy faithfulness" (Lamentations 3:22-23 RSV).

The main book in the Bible that teaches the holiness of God is the book of Leviticus. Yet even this book strongly speaks of God's love. Leviticus 19:18 says, "You shall not take vengeance or bear any grudge against the sons of your own people, but you shall love your neighbor as yourself: I am the LORD" (RSV). We also read in Leviticus 19:34, "The stranger who sojourns with you shall be to you as the native among you, and you shall love him as yourself . . ." (RSV).

Now we see this same basic statement in the New Testament from Jesus, "You have heard that it has been said, 'You shall love your neighbor and hate your enemy.' But I say to you, love your enemies, bless those who curse you, do good to those who hate you, and pray for those who spitefully use you and persecute you, that you may be sons of your Father in heaven; for He makes His sun rise on the evil and on the good, and sends rain on the just and on the unjust. For if you love those who love you, what reward have you? Do not even the tax collectors do the same? And if you greet your brethren only, what do you do more than others? Do not even the tax collectors do so? Therefore you shall be perfect, just as your Father in heaven is perfect" (Matthew 5:43-48 NKJ).

Paul wrote in Ephesians 1:4 that God, ". . . [has chosen us] in Him [Christ] before the foundation of the world, that we should ·be holy and without blame before Him in love . . ." (NKJ).

We see from these and many other verses that God loved us before He ever even made us. So, you see, there's nothing we can do to try to earn His love. We simply repent of our sins and receive it. God's love for us has no beginning and no end. It is from everlasting to everlasting. He has revealed that love supremely in Jesus Christ.

Because God's love is eternal, Paul was able to write these words in Romans 8, "Who shall separate us from the love of Christ? Shall tribulation, or distress, or persecution, or famine, or nakedness, or peril, or sword? As it is written: 'For your sake we are killed all day long; We are accounted as sheep for the slaughter.' Yet in all these things we are more than conquerors through Him who loved us. For I am persuaded that neither death nor life, nor angels nor principalities nor powers, nor things present nor things to come, nor height nor depth, nor any other created thing, shall be able to separate us from the love of God which is Christ Jesus our Lord" (Romans 8:35-39 NKJ).

God's Love Is Infinite

God's love is also *infinite*. As we've learned, this means limitless, boundless and measureless. Our love is constantly fluctuating. Sometimes we love someone more than we do at other times. But then sometimes we love a person less than we do at other times. This is because our love is influenced by the object of our love.

But God doesn't add to or take away from His love. He doesn't love us more at times than He does at other times. Nor does he love us less at times than He does at other times. *So there is nothing you can do to make God love you any more than He does already. Likewise, there is nothing you can do that will cause God to love you any less than He does already.* We can find rest in God's infinite love.

God's Love Is Uncaused

God's love is also different from human love in that God's love is *uncaused*. When we love someone it's because we find something that we believe is lovable in the one we love. The person becomes the object of our love. But the love we have for that person is because of something in that person that we think is lovable. That which we think is lovable calls forth love out of us.

There are two kinds of human love that can be called forth out of us. These are physical love and soulish love. We are now going to briefly discuss these two kinds of love.

Physical Love

Because of our fallen nature, human love is usually first manifested at the *physical level*. I'm sure you are aware that our first impressions of people are normally based on what they look like. People naturally don't enjoy being around others whose appearance is unpleasant to them. For example, a young man's attention is directed towards a young woman who, in the eyes of the young man, is physically attractive and pleasant to look at and admire. He takes notice of her. And when he sees such a woman, natural physical desires that God has built in him come forth. He wants to observe her more closely. Now all young ladies know this instinctively. So the woman, having these same natural desires, makes herself attractive for the young man whom she finds to be physically pleasant.

God has intended that a man and woman marry each other and come together in physical union and unity. As we read in Genesis 2, "And Adam said, 'This is now bone of my bone And flesh of my flesh; She shall be called Woman, Because she was taken out of Man.' Therefore a man shall leave his father and mother and be joined to his wife, and they shall become one flesh" (23-24 NKJ). So as we all know, physical love pertains to the body. The Greeks used the word "eros" to refer to physical love.

Soulish Love

The second manifestation of human love is at the *soulish level*. The soul is the invisible you that lives inside your body. It consists of your mind, emotions and will. When God created Adam, He breathed the breath of life into him and man became a living soul (Genesis 2:7). God then stated that it was not good for man to live alone because he requires fellowship (Genesis 2:18).

We often think of our soul in terms of our personality. Our personality expresses our individual uniqueness; it's what makes us different. So we all have different personalities. And even though we all have a need for fellowship, we don't like to be around people whom we believe to have an unpleasant personality. We like to be with people whom we think are pleasant.

When a young man and woman are attracted to each other

139

physically, they begin to spend time together. During this period, they begin to discover each other's personality. They may discover that they can't get along as well as they would like. They may have what we often refer to as a "personality conflict." But they may find that they are not only attracted to each other physically, but they also love each other's soul. Therefore, their desire to be in each other's company grows. Finally, they may decide that they would rather be with each other than anyone else.

So we see there is something we believe to be lovable about another person's soul that calls forth our soulish love so that we desire fellowship with certain people. *The Greeks used the word "phileo" to refer to this soulish kind of love.* Both "eros" love and "phileo" love are awakened and aroused by something we believe to be lovable in another person. Therefore, human love is a caused love called forth by an external object.

Agape Love

God's love is different from human love in that it is uncaused. God does not love out of passion or emotion. God loves because love is who God is in His being. It is His nature to love. *This means that God's love has nothing to do with the object of His love.* It is not a "called out" love based on the lovableness of an external object. God loves the unlovable as well as the lovable because God is love. In fact, in God's eyes, all of us are unlovable. We are all unlovable because we have all sinned and come short of His glory.

What good thing does God see in sinners that could call forth His love? What lovable thing in us could attract the heart of God? Paul wrote in Romans 7:18, "For I know that nothing good dwells within me . . ." (RSV). By this, Paul meant that everything he did was tainted by sin. And as we've learned, God hates sin, yet He loves the sinner. He loves us even in our sins because He Himself is eternal, infinite, uncaused love. Paul said it this way, "But God demonstrates His own love toward us, in that while we were still sinners, Christ died for us" (Romans 5:8 NKJ).

God loved Israel when they were still in their sins. (See Ezekiel 16.) He reminded them of His love when He brought them out of Egypt. Moses wrote, "The LORD did not set his affection on you and choose you because you were more numerous than other peoples, for you were the fewest of all peoples. But it was because the LORD loved you and kept the oath he swore to your forefathers that he brought you out with a mighty hand and redeemed you from the land of slavery, from the power of Pharaoh king of Egypt" (Deuteronomy 7:7-8 NIV).

God loves the Gentiles in their sin. Paul wrote in Ephesians, "But God, who is rich in mercy, because of His great love with which He loves us, even when we were dead in trespasses, made us alive together with Christ . . ." (Ephesians 2:4-5 NKJ).

Finally, *God loves the world in its sin.* For we learn in John 3:16-17, "For God so loved the world that He gave His only begotten Son, that whoever believes in Him should not perish but have everlasting life. For God did not send His Son into the world to condemn the world, but that the world through Him might be saved" (NKJ).

We learn further in 1 John, "In this the love of God was manifested towards us, that God has sent His only begotten Son into the world, that we might live through Him. In this is love, not that we loved God, but that He loved us and sent His Son to be the propitiation [sin-bearer] for our sins . . . We love Him because He first loved us" (4:9-10, 19 NKJ).

There is no reason for God's love towards us except Himself. This is a love for the spirit of a person. It's an uncaused, unconditional love. This kind of love was unknown to man so that Greeks had to make up a brand new word to describe it. They called it "agape" love. This is God's kind of love that is freely given without any consideration of the lovableness or merit of its object. And as we've just been reading, this love includes its enemies as well as its friends.

God's Love Through Us

I'm sure we all realize that this is the kind of love we need.

141

But how can we have this kind of love? Paul gives the answer in his letter to the Romans. He writes ". . . The love of God has been poured out in our hearts by the Holy Spirit who was given to us" (Romans 5:5 NKJ).

You see, we receive God's love into our hearts when we receive God Himself into our hearts. Jesus sent the Holy Spirit to come and live in us. The Holy Spirit will then love through us with God's agape love. It's not so much that we get love, but we get God who is love. We really don't need to pray for more of God's love. We just need to surrender to that love He has already given us through the Holy Spirit who lives in us.

Now this was not a new idea that Paul was presenting. The first thing God told the Hebrews when He brought them out of Egypt was that they were to love Him with all their heart, with all their soul and with all their might (Deuteronomy 6:5). But no one could do that with their own inadequate human love. So God told them how they could do it. He said, "And the LORD your God will circumcise your heart and the heart of your offspring, so that you will love the LORD your God with all your heart and with all your soul, that you may live" (Deuteronomy 30:6 RSV).

What God called a circumcision of the heart in the Old Testament, He calls being born again in the New Testament. (See Deuteronomy 10:16; Jeremiah 4:4; 9:25-26; John 3:3-7; Romans 2:29; Philippians 3:3.) *This is a divine cutting away of that imperfect human love and replacing it with God's love.*

One of the religious leaders came to Jesus with the following question, " 'Teacher, which is the greatest commandment in the law?' Jesus said to him, ' "You shall love the Lord your God with all your heart, with all your soul, and with all your mind." This is the first and great commandment. And the second is like it; "You shall love your neighbor as yourself." On these two commandments hang all the Law and the Prophets' " (Matthew 22:36-40 NKJ).

In John 14:23, Jesus said, ". . . If anyone loves Me, he will keep My word; and My Father will love Him, and We will come to him and make Our home with him" (NKJ). Jesus and the Father make their home with us through the person of the indwelling Holy Spirit. *The Holy Spirit loves through us with the uncaused love of God.* This is why Jesus said, "A new commandment I give to you, that you love one another; as I have loved you, that you also love one another. By this all will know that you are My disciples, if you have love for one another" (John 13:34-35 NKJ).

Jesus impressed this on us again in John 15. He said, "As the Father loved Me, I also have loved you; abide in My love. If you keep My commandments, you will abide in My love, just as I have kept My Father's commandments and abide in His love . . . . This is My commandment, that you love one another as I have loved you" (9-12 NKJ).

John wrote in 1 John, "Beloved, if God so loved us, we also ought to love one another. No one has seen God at any time. If we love one another, God abides in us, and His love has been perfected in us. By this we know that we abide in Him, and He in us, because He has given us of His spirit . . . . And we have known and believed the love that God has for us. God is love, and he who abides in love abides in God, and God in him . . . . If someone says, 'I love God,' and hates his brother, he is a liar; for he who does not love his brother whom he has seen, how can he love God whom he has not seen? And this commandment we have from Him: that he who loves God must love his brother also" (4:11-13, 16, 20-21 NKJ).

Yes, God is love. Do you know that love through Jesus Christ? Ask God to give you a revelation of it right at this moment. Then, by faith, simply receive that which God shows you. If you know that love, are you walking in it? *The only way the world will know that God is love is by seeing it lived out in you.* So we close this chapter with a final word from John. He writes to us, "My little children, let us not love in word or in tongue, but in deed and in truth" (1 John 3:18 NKJ).

Chapter 12—God Is Love

Review Exercise 11

1. How is God's love a holy love?

2. Explain the following types of love:

    a. *Eros*—

    b. *Phileo*—

    c. *Agape*—

3. How is God's love seen in His people?

4. How can you apply this knowledge to your life?

13

God Is Just

Perhaps nothing angers us more than seeing someone being treated unjustly. This is particularly true if that someone happens to be us. On the other hand, we don't like to see people get away with something when they deserve punishment. We like to see justice done, unless, of course, we happen to be the person deserving the punishment. Then we want mercy. We want justice for everyone else but mercy for ourselves. In this chapter, we're going to learn that God is just, yet He has made a way to administer His justice with mercy.

In Psalms 97:1-2 we read, "The LORD reigns; let the earth rejoice; let the many coastlands be glad! Clouds and thick darkness are round about him; righteousness and justice are the foundation of his throne" (RSV). This verse tells us that God rules over His creation with perfect justice and righteousness.

Moses wrote of God, "He is the Rock, His work is perfect; For all His ways are justice, A God of truth and without injustice; Righteous and upright [just] is He" (Deuteronomy 32:4 NKJ).

God reveals Himself in the Bible to be a just and righteous God. As with His other attributes, justice and righteousness is not something God does or has, but it is who He is in His very being. God in His nature is just and righteous.

Now when the Bible was translated into English, the same Hebrew and Greek word was translated as both justice and righteousness. So for practical purposes, the two words have the same meaning and I will be using them interchangeably.

Justice and righteousness is the attribute of God out of which God gives us exactly what we deserve. *God always does the right thing by us, and He Himself is the standard of what is right.* Now this can be terribly threatening to us, because deep down inside we all know we deserve God's wrath. Yet, as we will see, God's goodness complements His justice so that we are not all doomed to hell. Likewise, His love complements His holiness so that we may live in heaven.

God's Righteousness Is Different from Ours

God's righteousness is perfect as He is perfect. Psalms 92:15 tells us that there is no unrighteousness in God. Now what human can say this about himself? Well, of course, none of us can. We would like to think this is true about ourselves, but we know that it isn't. There is unrighteousness in each of us. We don't always do right. The Bible says that in God's sight, there is none righteous (Psalms 14:3, 53:3; Romans 3:10). The Bible says that our unrighteousness is sin and that sin separates us from God.

So there are two kinds of righteousness, God's and ours. God's is perfect while ours is imperfect, being tainted by sin. Our self-righteousness is like filthy rags when compared to God's righteousness (Isaiah 64:6). Yet, we like to think that our self-righteousness is good enough to save us from our sins. So we deceive ourselves by comparing ourselves to our neighbor. And if we look long enough and hard enough, we can always find some gross neighbor to compare ourselves to who will make us look pretty good.

We are like doodlebugs. Do you know that doodlebugs always compare themselves to each other. And, except for a few real gross doodlebugs, a doodlebug looks pretty good when compared to another doodlebug. But doodlebugs never compare themselves to humans. And we know why, don't we? Because every time a doodlebug compares himself to a human he loses. He comes up short everytime. We are just like doodlebugs, always comparing ourselves to each other. And except for those few gross neighbors who can only compare themselves to doodlebugs, we look pretty good compared to our neighbor. *But God doesn't compare us to each other. God compares us to Himself and, compared to Him, we always lose. We fall short of His glory every time.* (Romans 3:23.)

Now God doesn't want us to have this doodlebug syndrome. He told the Hebrews that He was going to destroy their enemies and give them a land. But He wanted them to know that it wasn't because of their righteousness. God said, "Do not say in your heart, after the LORD your God has thrust them out before you, 'It is because of my righteousness that the LORD has brought me in to possess this land'; whereas it is because of the wickedness of these nations that the LORD is driving them out before you. Not because of your righteousness or the uprightness of your heart are you going in to possess their land; but because of the wickedness of these nations the LORD your God is driving them out from before you, and that he may confirm the word which the LORD swore to your fathers, to Abraham, to Isaac, and to Jacob. Know therefore, that the LORD your God is not giving you this good land to possess because of your righteousness; for you are a stubborn people" (Deuteronomy 9:4-6 RSV).

Later, while in Babylonian exile, the Prophet Daniel wrote, "O my God, incline thy ear and hear; open thy eyes and behold our desolations, and the city which is called by thy name; for we do not present our supplications before thee on the ground of our righteousness, but on the ground of thy great mercy (Daniel 9:18 RSV).

The Apostle Paul expressed this same thought in the New Testament by writing that we are saved, "not by works of righteousness which we have done, but according to His mercy He saved us, by the washing of regeneration and renewing of the Holy Spirit, whom He poured out on us abundantly through Jesus Christ our Savior . . ." (Titus 3:5-6 NKJ).

The Bible very clearly tells us that we do not approach God through our own righteousness but through His, made available to us through the cross of Jesus Christ. We are now going to examine four aspects of God's justice and righteousness and how they apply to our lives today.

God's Ways Are Just and Right

First of all, God is just and right in the *way or manner in which He does things.* David and Bathsheba had a child born in adultery, and God took that child's life. To some, this might seem unfair of God. After all, the child was innocent in this situation. However, God showed mercy on the one who needed it the most (David), not the one who didn't (the child). So if there was anyone who had a right to question God, it was David. Yet David say, "The LORD is righteous in all His ways, Gracious [holy] in all His works" (Psalms 145:17 NKJ).

Hosea's wife was a prostitute who bore Hosea children from other men. Now Hosea was a prophet of God. And it certainly seems to us that God was unfair to Hosea by giving him an unfaithful wife. Yet Hosea wrote, ". . . The ways of the LORD are right; The righteous walk in them, But transgressors stumble in them" (Hosea 14:9 NKJ).

We often question God's ways, don't we? We accuse God of being unfair, unjust. We sometimes think He gives us a bad deal. We often point a finger at God and say, "Why did you allow this to happen to me?" I did this many times before I learned that God is perfectly just. *He always deals with us in a fair, equitable way.* That is the only way He can deal with us because that is His nature. God will never "set us up" as do some of our "friends." He will always deal with us according to His perfect, righteous nature.

Now God doesn't always tell us why He does the things He does. Furthermore, God doesn't owe us an explanation. As the sovereign God of the universe, God can do whatsoever He pleases. This could be very frightening. But for those who know God it is very comforting, because God always pleases to do right. He can't do otherwise because there is no unrighteousness in Him. *When we come to know God in His justice and righteousness, we can rest in Him and not worry about why He is doing something or the way in which He is doing it.*

God's Laws Are Just and Right

Next, we learn from the Bible that God's *laws* are just and right. Psalms 19:7-8 reads, "The law of the LORD is perfect, converting the soul; The testimony of the LORD is sure, making wise the simple; The statutes of the LORD are right . . ." (NKJ).

God Himself is the standard of what is right. But we can't see God. Therefore, He has revealed the nature of His righteous character to us through the Ten Commandments and other laws that He gave the Hebrews as a means to govern themselves. *God's laws reflect His character.* Through them, we learn that He is perfectly just and righteous. God's laws come from His spoken word, so we read, ". . . The word of the LORD is right . . ." (Psalms 33:4 NKJ).

God's laws are just and right because He is just and right. And if man will keep God's laws, there will be justice and righteousness on the earth. There will be right relationships between God and man, and man and man. It is for this reason that God told the Hebrews to appoint judges and administrators to govern the cities. Then God said, ". . . they shall judge the people with just judgment" (Deuteronomy 16:18 NKJ).

God wanted His just and right character to be seen through His people as they lived according to His just and right laws. Unfortunately, the Hebrews failed to do this. God then raised up prophets to warn them. God spoke these words to the king through the prophet Jeremiah ". . . Do justice and righteousness, and deliver from the hand of the oppressor him who has been robbed. And do no wrong or violence to the alien, the fatherless, and the widow, nor shed innocent blood in this place" (Jeremiah 22:3 RSV).

Ezekiel said to the rulers of Israel, ". . . Put away violence and oppression, and execute justice and righteousness . . ." (Ezekiel 45:9 RSV).

The Hebrews were not living in a just and right relationship with God nor with each other. Yet all the while, they brought their sacrifices to the Temple and put on a religious show for God. They thought that they could stay in God's favor by going through their religious ritual, even though they were unjust in their dealings with one another.

God, however, was not impressed by their meaningless religious ritual. He was interested in an inward righteousness of the heart. David understood this and prayed, "O let the evil of the wicked come to an end, but establish thou the righteous, thou who triest the minds and hearts, thou righteous God. My shield is with God, who saves the upright in heart" (Psalms 7:9-10 RSV).

We read in Psalms 15:1-2, "LORD, who may abide in your tabernacle? Who may dwell in Your holy hill? He who walks uprightly, And works righteousness, And speaks the truth in his heart" (NKJ). But the people didn't listen to God's call for righteousness. Isaiah said, "No one calls for justice . . ." (Isaiah 59:4 NKJ).

God then raised up more prophets to remind the people that He was interested in the condition of their heart. God spoke through the Prophet Amos, "I hate, I despise your feasts, and I take no delight in your solemn assemblies. Even though you offer me your burnt offerings and cereal offerings, I will not accept them, and the peace offerings of your fatted beasts I will not look upon. Take away from me

150

the noise of your songs; to the melody of your harps I will not listen. But let justice roll down like waters, and righteousness like an everflowing stream" (Amos 5:21-24 RSV).

Through the Prophet Micah, the question was asked of God, "With what shall I come before the LORD and bow down before the exalted God? Shall I come before him with burnt offerings . . .?" (Micah 6:6 NIV). Micah responded, "Will the LORD be pleased with thousands of rams, with ten thousand rivers of oil? Shall I offer my firstborn for my transgression, the fruit of my body for the sin of my soul? He has showed you, O man, what is good. And what does the LORD require of you? To act justly and to love mercy and to walk humbly with your God" (Micah 6:7-8 NIV).

After all these warnings, the Hebrews still refused to heed God's call to righteousness. Finally, it became necessary for Him to judge them. His judgment came in the form of allowing enemy nations to conquer the land and take the people captive. But even in their judgment, God gave the Hebrews a message of hope. Jeremiah prophesied, " 'Behold, the days are coming,' says the LORD, 'That I will raise to David a Branch of righteousness; A King shall reign and prosper, And execute judgment and righteousness in the earth. In His days Judah will be saved, And Israel will dwell safely: Now this is His name by which He will be called: THE LORD OUR RIGHTEOUSNESS' " (Jeremiah 23:5-6 NKJ).

According to this prophecy, the day would come when the Messiah would come into the world through the lineage of David. He would rule as King over all the earth. He would rule His kingdom with justice and righteousness and establish this same rule in the hearts of men.

God's Judgments Are Just and Right

Since the Hebrews rejected God's righteousness, they had to be judged. God's just and righteous nature requires Him to judge His creatures. Yet God's judgments are always consistent with His being. We learn from Psalms 119:137, "Righteous art thou, O LORD, and right are thy judgments" (RSV).

151

When Daniel was in captivity he wrote these words, "As it is written in the law of Moses, all this calamity has come upon us, yet we have not entreated the favor of the LORD our God, turning from our iniquities and giving heed to thy truth. Therefore the LORD has kept ready the calamity and has brought it upon us; for the LORD our God is righteous in all the works which he has done, and we have not obeyed his voice" (Daniel 9:13-14 RSV).

Nehemiah also wrote, "However You are just in all that has befallen us; For you have dealt faithfully, But we have done wickedly" (Nehemiah 9:33 NKJ).

God must judge us. His very nature demands it. *Yet it often seems that people get away with injustice and unrighteousness.* It seems that crime pays. We see evil people having it easy, while God's people suffer. We often think to ourselves, "Lord, what's the use of being good?" David questioned God about this in Psalms 73. God answered David by showing him that those who are unjust are standing in slippery places, and in due time they would fall into destruction.

We sometimes wonder if God is ever going to do anything to right the wrongs in the world. Well, God assures us that He is going to do something. But He also tells us that He is longsuffering, plenteous in mercy, slow to anger and not willing that any should perish (2 Peter 3:9).

God says in Ezekiel 33:11, ". . . I have no pleasure in the death of the wicked, but that the wicked turn from his way and live; turn back, turn back from your evil ways; for why will you die, O house of Israel?" (RSV). God does not take pleasure in the death of the wicked. In the end, justice and righteousness will prevail.

God's just and righteous nature is our guarantee that all wrongs will be made right. We read in Ecclesiastes 3:17, ". . . God will judge the righteous and the wicked, for he has appointed a time for every matter, and for every work" (RSV). We also learn in Ecclesiastes 11:9, "Rejoice, O young man, in your youth, and let your heart cheer you in the days of your youth; walk in the ways of your heart and the sight of your eyes. But know that for all these things God will bring you into judgment" (RSV). Ecclesiastes 12:14 warns us, "For God will bring every work into judgment, Including every secret thing, Whether it is good or whether it is evil" (NKJ).

David wrote these words about God's judgment. "The righteous shall rejoice when he sees the vengeance; He shall wash his feet in the blood of the wicked, So that men will say, 'Surely there is a reward for the righteous; Surely He is God who judges in the earth' " (Psalms 58:10-11 NKJ).

God's Wrath Is Righteous

The fourth aspect of God's righteousness is His *wrath*. We don't like to talk about God's wrath. We think that "wrath" is beneath God's divine dignity. We think this way because we have a human view of God's wrath. Human wrath usually results from a loss of self-control. It's a passing situation. It is a striking back out of wounded pride.

But God's wrath is not like ours. *God's wrath is an outpouring of His holy anger against injustice and unrighteousness.* It is not a passing emotion. Psalms 119:142 tells us, "Your righteousness is an everlasting righteousness . . ." (NKJ). We learn in Numbers 14:18, "The LORD is long-suffering and abundant in mercy, forgiving iniquity and transgression; but He by no means clears the guilty . . ." (NKJ).

We should be grateful for God's wrath. We sure wouldn't want a God who was indifferent to injustice and unrighteousness. It wouldn't be a very good God who allowed evil people to go unpunished and to end up in the same place as people who love righteousness. This certainly would not be a good God. Even in our sins, we know it's not right for the bad guys to win.

So the Bible speaks of God's wrath and His goodness in the same breath. The Prophet Nahum wrote, "The LORD is a jealous God and avenging, the LORD is avenging and wrathful; the LORD takes vengeance on his adversaries and keeps wrath for his enemies. The LORD is slow to anger and of great might, and the LORD will by no means clear the

153

guilty. Who can stand before his indignation? Who can endure the heat of his anger? His wrath is poured out like fire . . ."(Nahum 1:2-3, 6 RSV). Nahum then says, "The Lord is good, a stronghold in the day of trouble; he knows those who take refuge in him. But with an overflowing flood we will make a full end of his adversaries, and will pursue his enemies into darkness" (Nahum 1:7-8 RSV).

Ezra wrote, ". . . The hand of our God is upon all those for good who seek Him, but His power and His wrath are against all those who forsake Him" (Ezra 8:22 NKJ). David said, "The LORD preserves all who love him; but all the wicked he will destroy" (Psalms 145:20 RSV).

God's first intention toward us is love, but if we continue to refuse His love, we will fall under His wrath. The writer of Chronicles says it this way, "The LORD, the God of their fathers, sent persistently to them by his messengers, because he had compassion on his people and on his dwelling place; but they kept mocking the messengers of God, despising his words, and scoffing at his prophets, till the wrath of the LORD rose against his people, till there was no remedy" (2 Chronicles 36:15-16 RSV).

We learn from this statement that the Hebrews' hearts became so hard, that God, in His all knowledge, realized that they would never turn back to Him. So there was no further use for Him to be patient with them.

God gave this same word to Jeremiah. He said, "I have made you a tester of metals and my people the ore, that you may observe and test their ways. They are all hardened rebels, going out to slander. They are bronze and iron; they all act corruptly. The bellows blow fiercely to burn away the lead with fire, but the refining goes on in vain; the wicked are not purged out. They are called rejected silver, because the LORD has rejected them" (Jeremiah 6:27-30 NIV).

God's righteous judgment begins on a nation and an individual when He gives them over to their own sins. (See Romans 1-2.) And because God is eternal in His being, this judgment will continue throughout all eternity. Those who find themselves in hell will bear in their body the sum total of all their sins—forever (2 Corinthians 5:10).

Jesus Our Righteousness

But now we have a problem. We learned earlier in this chapter that God saves the "upright in heart." Yet we also discovered that none of us are upright in heart. How, then, can we be with God? This dooms all of us to God's wrath. *The question that all religions seek to answer is, "How can we escape God's wrath?"* All religions of the world, except Christianity, answer this by saying, "You escape God's wrath through your own self-righteousness (works)." But the Bible (and Christianity) says, "Man's self-righteousness falls short of God's absolute, divine standards. Therefore, only God Himself can provide us with the kind of righteousness we need."

But how does God accomplish this? The Apostle Paul tells us with these words, "While we were yet helpless, at the right time Christ died for the ungodly. Why, one will hardly die for a righteous man—though perhaps for a good man one will dare even to die. But God shows his love for us in that while we were yet sinners Christ died for us. Since, therefore, we are now justified by his blood, much more shall we be saved by him from the wrath of God" (Romans 5:6-9 RSV). (See also 1 Thessalonians 1:10, 5:9; Revelation 6:15-17.)

Paul explains in these verses how we are saved from the wrath of God. He says it is by being justified by the blood of Christ. The word "justified" means to be declared righteous. We read in 1 John 2:1, ". . . If anyone sins, we have an Advocate with the Father, Jesus Christ the righteous" (NKJ).

Jesus is the Lord our righteousness of whom Jeremiah spoke. He was the righteous branch of David who lived a perfect life never committing one single unrighteous act. *And when you accept Him as the one who died for your sins, God credits the perfect righteousness of Jesus Christ to your spiritual bank account.* As we learn from 1 John 1:9, "If we confess our sins, He is faithful and just to forgive us our sins and to cleanse us from all unrighteousness" (NKJ).

We also read in 2 Corinthians 5:21, "For He [God] made Him [Jesus] who knew no sin to be sin for us, that we might become the righteousness of God in Him" (NKJ).

Righteousness Imputed

This is what it means to be declared righteous by God. We often speak of this as an imputed righteousness because the word imputed is an ancient business term which simply means to credit you with something that you don't have yourself. You and I do not have perfect righteousness, but Jesus does. So God imputes, or credits, Jesus' righteousness to your spiritual bank account, thus saving you from God's wrath against unrighteousness. *This is what makes Christianity different from all other religions of the world.* (See also Galatians 2:16; Philippians 3:9.)

When Isaiah thought of this imputed righteousness he wrote, "I will greatly rejoice in the LORD, My soul shall be joyful in my God For He has clothed me with the garments of salvation, He has covered me with the robe of righteousness . . ." (Isaiah 61:10 NKJ).

Righteousness Imparted

So we see that God doesn't want us to be "religious"; He wants us to be "righteous." He has declared us to be righteous through Jesus Christ. This is our position in Christ. This is wonderful news and cause for rejoicing. We no longer feel we must run from God and bear the burden of guilt for our sins. God has forgiven our sins and no longer remembers them. He has separated us from them as far as the east is from the west. He has cast them into the sea of forgetfulness. This is indeed the Good News!

Now it is one thing to be declared righteous, but living and acting righteously is an entirely different matter. It's great that God has declared us to be righteous. But wouldn't it also be great if somehow, God could help us to live righteously? Well, God can and God has provided this help so that we can actually live up to what God says about us.

God has provided this help for us by giving us the Holy Spirit. Now, as we've learned, the Holy Spirit is God Himself coming to live His own divine life in us and through us. So when we allow the Holy Spirit to control our lives, the very righteousness of Jesus Christ will be manifested, or seen,

156

in us. We often speak of this as imparted righteousness because we actually receive it into ourselves.

God said it this way through the Prophet Ezekiel, "Then I will give them one heart, and I will put a new spirit within them, and take the stony heart out of their flesh, and give them a heart of flesh, that they may walk in My statutes and keep My judgments and do them; and they shall be My people, and I will be their God" (Ezekiel 11:19-20 NKJ). (See also Ezekiel 36:25-27.)

The Apostle John wrote, "If you know that He is righteous, you know that everyone who practices righteousness is born of Him" (1 John 2:29 NKJ). *When the world sees God's righteousness in His people, they will know that He is righteous and that His righteousness is different.* They will realize that they can no longer try to approach God through their own self-righteousness. They will realize that God's absolute divine righteousness is beyond them but is available to them through Jesus Christ, the Lord our righteousness.

Yes, God's perfect righteousness is available to you for the asking. He desires to clothe you with His garment of salvation and robe of righteousness. He will give you the power to walk in that righteousness through His Spirit. As Jesus said, "Blessed are those who hunger and thirst for righteousness, For they shall be filled" (Matthew 5:6 NKJ).

Chapter 13—God Is Just

Review Exercise 12

1. What do we mean when we say that God is just?

2. List four aspects of God that reveal His justice.

   a.

   b.

   c.

   d.

3. How can God show us mercy without violating His justice?

4. How can you apply this knowledge to your life?

14
God Is Good

The last moral attribute of God that we are going to learn about is that God is good. The Bible is full of statements that speak about the goodness of God. I think you will find Psalms 107 to be particularly encouraging. It begins with these words, "Oh, give thanks to the LORD, for He is good! For His mercy endures forever" (Psalms 107:1 NKJ).

Only in the Bible do we find the revelation that the creator God is a good God. All the false gods which man has made with his own hands are, in some measure, cruel gods that man must cringe before. I've observed that we sometimes like this false image of God, because, if we convince ourselves that God is cruel, we can justify our running away from Him.

But people fear God for the wrong reason. In their guilt of sin, they are afraid of God because they think that He is cruel and wants to punish them. And they know they deserve to be punished. So they try to run from God. Yet the whole time they are running, God is saying, "I am good. Come to me so I can bless you out of My goodness." To everyone who has ever been afraid of God, David wrote, "O taste and see that the Lord is good!" (Psalms 34:8 RSV).

God Alone Is Good

What does the Bible mean when it says that God is good? A reasonable definition is that *God's goodness is His steadfast lovingkindness and goodwill towards His creatures.*

Because God is good, He naturally wants to bless us. It is His nature to bless. We humans, on the other hand, don't naturally want to bless others with lovingkindness and goodwill. Anyone who thinks that man is basically good hasn't read the paper in a long, long time, the last six thousand years to be specific. *Unfortunately, we are not warm, goodhearted creatures with just a few little wrinkles that need to be ironed out.*

Man is basically selfish. We have to work at being good because it's definitely not our nature. If you are still blinded by that deception, let me ask you the following question: "Do you teach your children how to be bad, or do you teach them how to be good?" Now any honest parent can immediately answer this question without any help. We have to teach our children how to be good, don't we? They know how to be bad; it's their nature.

One time a man came to Jesus and called Him "good Master." Jesus rebuked him and said, "why are you calling me good? Only God is good" (Matthew 19:17). Jesus was trying to get the man to realize who he was talking to. He meant that only God is naturally good.

Goodness is who God is in His very essence and being. God doesn't try to be good; He is good. *All that flows out of God is good.* Every good and perfect gift comes from Him who moves the course of world events for the good of those who love Him and have been called according to His purpose. (See Romans 8:28; James 1:17.) After meditating on all that God has done for him, the Psalmist wrote,

160

". . . Oh, give thanks to the LORD, for He is good! For His mercy endures forever" (Psalms 106:1 NKJ).

God's Goodness Is Eternal and Infinite

Many people seem to think that the God of the Old Testament is cruel but that somehow He changed to become a good God in the New Testament. But of course, we've learned that this cannot be true because God's goodness is eternal and infinite. God has always wanted to shower His creatures with lovingkindness and goodwill.

Now we are very moody creatures. Our disposition is constantly changing. We're never sure just how to approach people because we don't know what kind of mood they are in. We don't know if they're going to be in a good mood or a bad mood. But we don't have this problem with God. *God is always in a "good mood."* Psalms 52:1 says, ". . . The goodness of God endures continually" (NKJ). So you see, we don't have to wait until God gets in a good mood to approach Him. God is always in a good mood.

And you know, God is not more good now than He was in the past. Likewise, He is not going to be more good in the future than He is now. God Himself is eternal infinite goodness. Now to help us understand God's goodness, let's look closely at four ways He has revealed it to us.

God's Goodness in Creation

We first see God's goodness revealed in *creation.* Genesis 1:31 tells us, "Then God saw everything that He had made, and indeed, it was very good . . ." (NKJ). God could say that all of His creation was good because it was in perfect harmony with Himself and with each other. Everything that God made by the power of His spoken word was a reflection of His goodness.

For example, God made man with a wonderful body. Yet, our body is so complex, that we still know only a very little about how it works. God gave us a fantastic body, complete in itself, with every needed member in place and functioning automatically in perfect harmony with the other members.

161

David had these comments on the wonder of the human body, "For you created my inmost being; you knit me together in my mother's womb. I praise you because I am fearfully and wonderfully made; your works are wonderful, I know that full well" (Psalms 139:13-14 NIV).

God's goodness doesn't stop with man but extends beyond man to include all of His creation. We read in Psalms 145:15-16, "The eyes of all look to thee, and thou givest them their food in due season. Thou openest thy hand, thou satisfiest the desire of every living thing" (RSV). Psalms 136:25 says that God gives food to all flesh.

We learn in Psalms 104 that God placed springs in the valleys and streams in the mountains so that the birds and animals could have plenty of water to drink. He made the grass to grow for the beast of the field and fruits and vegetables from the land for man. God provided trees for the birds to make their nests and mountains for the wild goats. He provides meat for the young lions and all the fish of the sea depend on Him for their daily food. God opens wide His hand to feed them and they are satisfied with His bountiful provisions.

We see God's goodness in the variety of natural pleasures He has provided for us. God has not only given us our physical senses, but He also gratifies them for us. God could have made all food tasteless and it would still provide us with the nutrition our body needs. But God gave flavor to our food so it would be pleasing to taste. You know, every hot fudge sundae is a testimony to the goodness of God.

God could have made a dull, gray, blah world. But He clothed all of His creation with beautiful colors so it would be pleasing to look at. He could have made flowers without an aroma, but He gave them a sweet fragrance to delight our nostrils. He could have made birds that didn't sing, but their song is a melody to our ears. And the sensation of touch makes us feel loved and wanted and a part of all that God has created. The Psalmist was surely right when he wrote, ". . . The earth is full of the goodness of the LORD" (Psalms 33:5 NKJ).

God's Goodness in Dealing with Man

Next, we see God's goodness in His *dealings with man.* Moses had learned much about God as He brought the Hebrews out of Egypt. He saw God's justice in delivering the Hebrews from slavery. He observed God's power in the miracles that brought about the deliverance. He learned of God's holiness in the commandments and laws. But he had not yet seen God's goodness. This was a part of God's nature that Moses did not know about. But as they began their journey, God gives Moses a revelation of His goodness. God said to Moses, ". . . I will make all My goodness pass before you, and I will proclaim the name of the LORD before you. I will be gracious to whom I will be gracious, and I will have compassion on whom I will have compassion" (Exodus 33:19 NKJ).

This was like God saying to Moses, "I am going to show you something about Myself that is going to blow your mind. I'm going to show you something you've never thought of. I'm going to show that the living God is a good God full of lovingkindness and goodwill towards His creatures."

Then God explains His goodness to Moses. We read the following account, "Then the LORD descended in the cloud and stood with him there, and proclaimed the name of the LORD. And the LORD passed before him and proclaimed, 'The LORD, the LORD God, merciful and gracious, long-suffering, and abounding in goodness and truth, keeping mercy for thousands, forgiving iniquity and transgression and sin, by no means clearing the guilty, visiting the iniquity of the fathers upon the children and the children's children to the third and fourth generation' " (Exodus 34:5-7 NKJ).

This account tells us that God proclaimed His name to Moses. In Bible times, a person's name revealed his character and nature. So when God says He is going to proclaim His name, it means He's going to show Moses something about His character and nature. God then proclaims that He is good. *He says that His goodness includes mercy, grace, long-suffering and truth.* Let's now briefly examine each of these.

163

God's Mercy

Mercy is the aspect of God's goodness out of which He shows compassion towards His creatures. In 2 Corinthians 1:3, Paul refers to God as the "Father of mercies." God's holiness says, "The penalty for sin is death." God's justice says, "The penalty must be paid." God's mercy says, "I don't want you to pay it." God's love says, "I'll come to earth and pay it for you." This is how God deals with sin in perfect harmony with Himself.

God's mercy extends to all of His creation. We read in Psalms 119:64, "The earth, O LORD, is full of Your mercy . . ." (NKJ). Psalms 145:8-9 tells us, "The LORD is gracious and full of compassion, Slow to anger and great in mercy. The LORD is good to all, And His tender mercies are over all His works" (NKJ).

Since God is eternal, all aspects of His goodness are eternal. We read in Psalms 118:29, "Oh, give thanks to the LORD, for He is good! For His mercy endures forever" (NKJ). Psalms 100:5 says, "For the LORD is good; His mercy is everlasting, And His truth endures to all generations" (NKJ). Jeremiah wrote, "Through the LORD'S mercies we are not consumed, Because His compassions fail not. They are new every morning; Great is Your faithfulness" (Lamentations 3:22-23 NKJ).

God's mercy is eternal, but we must understand this in light of God's justice, which is also eternal. *This means that we must accept God's mercy through Jesus Christ in this present life. You see, God cannot show mercy beyond the grave to those who have rejected it during their lifetime because this would require Him to violate His eternal justice. This is why it does no good to have some kind of religious ceremony or prayers for the dead.* People who presume upon God's mercy will eventually come under His wrath, which we learned in a previous chapter, is also eternal. Isaiah said it this way, ". . . It is a people of no understanding; Therefore He who made them will not have mercy on them, And He who formed them will show them no favor" (Isaiah 27:11 NKJ).

Yes, God's mercy is everlasting, but it is only extended beyond the grave to those who respond to Him in this life. We learn this over and over in the Bible. Psalms 86:5 reads, ". . . You, LORD, are good, and ready to forgive, And abundant in mercy to all those who call upon You" (NKJ). We learn in Psalms 103, "For as the heavens are high above the earth, So great is His mercy toward those who fear Him . . . . But the mercy of the LORD is from everlasting to everlasting On those who fear Him . . . To such as keep His covenant, And to those who remember His commandments to do them" (Psalms 103:11, 17-18 NKJ).

God's Grace

God's grace is His unmerited favor. The Psalmists wrote of God's grace, ". . . The LORD is gracious and full of compassion" (Psalms 111:4 NKJ). We also read in Psalms 116:5, "Gracious is the LORD, and righteous; Yes, our God is merciful" (NKJ). God's mercy is offered to everyone, but His grace extends eternally only to those who respond to His mercy. We respond to God's mercy by turning from our sins and accepting His unmerited favor of salvation through Jesus Christ.

We read in 2 Chronicles 30:9, ". . . The LORD your God is gracious and merciful, and will not turn His face from you if you return to Him" (NKJ). The Prophet Joel wrote, " 'Now, therefore,' says the LORD, 'Turn to Me with all your heart, With fasting, with weeping, and with mourning.' So rend your heart and not your garments; Return to the LORD your God, For He is gracious and merciful, Slow to anger, and of great kindness . . ." (Joel 2:12-13 NKJ).

God's good grace is the means of our salvation, which is made effective for us through Jesus Christ. As Paul so well stated, ". . . By grace you have been saved through faith, and that not of yourselves; it is the gift of God, not of works, lest anyone should boast" (Ephesians 2:8-9 NKJ).

People often contrast God's law with God's grace. We are told that the Hebrews in the Old Testament were saved by keeping God's law while we in the New Testament are saved

165

by God's grace. *This is not a true statement.* We've always been saved by God's grace through faith in the innocent substitutionary sacrifice. *A more proper contrast between the Old Testament and the New Testament is law and Spirit, not law and grace. In the Old Testament, God gave the law as a revelation of His grace, while in the New Testament, He revealed His grace by giving the Spirit.*

God's Longsuffering

God's longsuffering is His goodness being patient with us. Psalms 86:15 reads, "But You, O LORD, are a God full of compassion, and gracious, Longsuffering and abundant in mercy and truth" (NKJ). Psalms 103:8 encourages us with these words, "The LORD is merciful and gracious, Slow to anger, and abounding in mercy" (NKJ). *God is patient with us and gives us every opportunity to accept His grace and be saved from our sins. Since God is just in His longsuffering, He gives everyone a fair opportunity. Oh, how we should praise God that He doesn't strike us all dead.*

But instead of praising God, the world thumbs its nose at God. It openly defies Him, as if daring Him to do anything about the way they live. Since God doesn't always instantly punish sinners, people think it's safe to do wrong. We learn this in Ecclesiastes 8:11 which says, "Because the sentence against an evil work is not executed speedily, therefore the heart of the sons of men is fully set in them to do evil" (NKJ). The reason God does not always execute judgment is because He is longsuffering. Peter said it this way, "The Lord is not slack concerning His promise, as some count slackness, but is longsuffering toward us, not willing that any should perish but that all should come to repentance" (2 Peter 3:9 NKJ).

God's longsuffering, however, is balanced by His justice. This means that there is a point in time, which only God knows, when your heart becomes so hardened, that God knows you are never going to receive Him. When you reach this point, God gives you up to your own lust.

This is just what happened in the days of Noah. The world

was turning its back on God. God warned them by saying that His Spirit would not always strive with them (Genesis 6:3). His longsuffering gave them another 120 years to repent, but they would not (Genesis 6:3). God then brought judgment against them with the great flood.

Romans 2:4-5 asks us to consider the following question, ". . . Do you presume upon the riches of his kindness and forbearance and patience? Do you not know that God's kindness is meant to lead you to repentance? But by your hard and impenitent heart you are storing up wrath for yourself on the day of wrath when God's righteous judgment will be revealed" (RSV). This is why the Bible says, ". . . Today, if you will hear His voice, Do not harden your hearts . . ." (Hebrews 3:15 NKJ).

God's Truth

When the Bible speaks of God being truth, it means that He is *reality*. David wrote, "Into Your hand I commit my spirit; You have redeemed me, O LORD God of truth" (Psalms 31:5 NKJ). The one true living God is the real thing; and everything else that is not in accordance with Him is false. Jesus said it in these words, "And this is eternal life, that they may know You, the only true God, and Jesus Christ whom You have sent" (John 17:3 NKJ). (See also John 8:26.)

Satan, on the other hand, is a liar and the truth is not in him (John 8:44). The Bible also calls Satan a deceiver (Revelation 12:9). Satan tries to deceive us by presenting his lies as truth. But his words and ways are false. Yet many people choose to believe his lies. The Bible says they walk in darkness and do not live according to the truth (1 John 1:6). Therefore, they cannot see things clearly. Their whole life is a lie. Paul said it this way, "For although they knew God they did not honor him as God or give thanks to him, but they became futile in their thinking and their senseless minds became darkened. Claiming to be wise, they became fools" (Romans 1:21-22 RSV). But when we come to know God, we can see things clearly and walk in light rather than darkness.

Since God is truth, everything that comes from Him is real. Psalms 33:4 reads, ". . . The word of the LORD is right, and all His work is done in truth" (NKJ). We learn in Psalms 119:160, "The entirety of Your word is truth . . ." (NKJ). *You can rely on what God does and what God says because He himself is truth.* For this reason, the Bible says that God cannot lie. (See Titus 1:2; Numbers 23:19; 1 Samuel 15:29.)

Since God is eternal, His truth endures forever (Psalms 117:2). *Whatever God has said in the past still holds true today and will hold true tomorrow.* The penalty for sin is still death and the gift of God is still eternal life through Jesus Christ our Lord (Romans 6:23).

God's Goodness in Jesus Christ

Thirdly, God has supremely revealed His goodness to us through the Lord Jesus Christ. It was said of Jesus in Acts 10:38 that, "He went about doing good." Well, of course He did. *He was goodness in the flesh.* Jesus was good by nature so that everything that flowed out of Him was good. He was the perfect revelation of God's steadfast lovingkindness of goodwill towards His creatures.

On one occasion, the religious leaders caught a woman in adultery. Now the penalty for adultery was stoning. So they brought her to Jesus to see what He would say concerning her. Jesus said to them, "He that is without sin among you, let him cast the first stone." The accusers left. Then Jesus turned to the woman and asked, "Where are your accusers? Who is it that condemns you?" The woman responded, "No one, Lord." Jesus said, "Neither do I accuse you; go and sin no more." (See John 8:1-11.)

Here was mercy in the flesh. The woman should have been put to death, but Jesus had compassion towards her. He didn't condemn her. He told her to go. But He also said, "And sin no more."

Jesus was speaking of God's *mercy* when he said, ". . . God did not send His Son into the world to condemn the world, but that the world through Him might be saved. He who believes in Him is not condemned; but he who does not believe is **condemned already**, because he has not believed in the name of the only begotten Son of God" (John 3:17-18 NKJ).

Jesus illustrated God's *grace* in the story of the prodigal son. (See Luke 15:11-32.) In this story, the son took his inheritance and squandered it foolishly in a far country. He finally ended up broke, and the only job he could get was feeding the pigs. While feeding the pigs, he realized that even his father's servants had it better than he did. So he came to his senses and headed home. When his father saw him coming down the road, he ran out to meet him. The son was not able to clean himself up before meeting his father. But the father accepted him just as he was in all his filth and stink. He gave his son a new suit, put a ring on his finger, shoes on his feet and killed the fatted calf.

And you know, we are just like this prodigal son. We've run from God and squandered away our life in the pleasures of the world. Yet God has come out to meet us in the person of Jesus of Nazareth. God has extended His unmerited favor to us. He accepts us just as we are right out of the pig pen of life. So you don't have to get cleaned up to come to God. You come to Him just as you are and He cleans you up by clothing you with His garment of salvation and robe of righteousness. This is God's grace made available to us through Jesus Christ.

Jesus showed us God's *longsuffering.* For example, His trials were a mockery. And the physical beatings He endured was beyond belief. First they stripped Him naked and laid 39 cruel lashes on Him that tore chunks of flesh out of His back. They spat in His face, pulled the hair out of His beard, struck Him with their open hand and then again with their fist. They hit Him on the head with a club and beat Him so badly that He was hardly recognizable as a human being. They pressed a crown of thorns on His head and mocked Him. Then they took Him and crucified Him. They did all of this even though the Roman governor said he could find no fault in Him. Yet in spite of this greatest of all injustices, the Bible says that Jesus opened not His mouth (Matthew 27:14).

Through Jesus we know the *truth* or reality of God. John said of Jesus that He was full of grace and truth (John 1:14). Jesus Himself said that He was the way, the truth and the life (John 14:6). He also promised to send the Holy Spirit whom He called the Spirit of Truth (John 16:13). The Holy Spirit would guide us into all truth and help us to see the reality of God in Jesus Christ. Paul then wrote that those who rejected this truth would be damned (2 Thessalonians 2:10-12).

So we see the goodness of God perfectly revealed in Jesus Christ. He is God's mercy, God's grace, God's longsuffering and God's truth. We can know that God is good in a very personal way by receiving the Spirit of Christ into our own life.

God's Goodness in Us

This brings us to the fourth way we can see God's goodness. *He reveals it through all of those who have received Him into their lives.* To all who claim the name of Christian, Jesus said, "Let your light so shine before men, that they may see your good works and glorify your Father in heaven" (Matthew 5:16 NKJ).

In that sermon Jesus said, "Blessed are the merciful, For they shall obtain mercy" (Matthew 5:7 NKJ). He then went on to say, "Therefore be merciful, just as your Father also is merciful" (Luke 6:36 NKJ).

Jesus spoke these words concerning God's grace, "You have heard that it was said, 'An eye for an eye and a tooth for a tooth.' But I tell you not to resist an evil person. But whoever slaps you on your right cheek, turn the other to him also. If anyone wants to sue you and take away your tunic, let him have your cloak also. And whoever compels you to go one mile, go with him two. Give to him who asks you, and from him who wants to borrow from you do not turn away. You have heard that it was said, 'You shall love your neighbor and hate your enemy.' But I say to you, love your enemies, bless those who curse you, do good to those who hate you, and pray for those who spitefully use you and persecute you, that you may be sons of your Father in heaven; for He makes His sun rise on the evil and on the good, and sends rain on the just and on the unjust" (Matthew 5:38-45 NKJ).

In regard to longsuffering, Jesus told Peter to forgive seventy times seven if necessary (Matthew 18:21-22). He also said, ". . . If you forgive men their trespasses, your heavenly Father will also forgive you. But if you do not forgive men their trespasses, neither will your Father forgive your trespasses" (Matthew 6:14-15 NKJ). Paul wrote that we should be longsuffering, bearing with one another in love (Ephesians 4:1-2).

Paul wrote to the Ephesians that we should "speak the truth in love" (Ephesians 4:15). John wrote that we should not love just in word or in tongue but also in deed and in truth (1 John 3:18). He said, that in this way, we would really know we have God's truth (Jesus) living in us (verse 19). In his third letter, John wrote, "I have no greater joy than to hear that my children walk in truth" (3 John 4 NKJ).

Do you know God's goodness through Jesus Christ? Once you have asked Him into your heart, you will never again be afraid of God. *As you come to know that goodness, let me encourage you to walk in it. As the world sees that goodness flowing out of you, they will stop running from God and come to the one who was goodness in the flesh.* The Apostle John gives us this final word, "Beloved, do not imitate what is evil, but what is good. He who does good is of God, but he who does evil has not seen God" (3 John 11 NKJ).

The Sum of it All

Yes, there is a God. He is the self-existing One who is eternal and infinite in all of His being. He is the personal Spirit who has revealed Himself to us as Father, Son and Holy Spirit. He is glorious in His majestic attributes and perfect in His moral character. And He wants us to know Him. When we see God for who He really is our only response can be that which was expressed by the Apostle Paul. He said, "But indeed I also count all things loss for the excellence of the knowledge of Christ Jesus my Lord, for whom I have suffered the loss of all things, and count them as rubbish, that I may gain Christ and be found in Him, not having my own righteousness, which is from the law, but that which is through faith in Christ, the righteousness which is from God by faith; that I may know Him and the power of His resurrection, and the fellowship of His sufferings, being conformed to His death, if, by any means, I may attain to the resurrection from the dead" (Philippians 3:8-11 NKJ).

Chapter 14—God Is Good

Review Exercise 13

1. What do we mean when we say that God is good?

2. List four ways that God has revealed His goodness to us.

   a.

   b.

   c.

   d.

3. How can God be good while at the same time allow His creatures to suffer so much?

4. How can you apply this knowledge to your life?

APPENDIX

SCRIPTURE REFERENCES

God Is Sovereign

Psalms 47:6-8—

Daniel 4:17—

Daniel 4:25—

Psalms 83:18—

Psalms 135:6-7—

Jeremiah 10:12-13—

Psalms 22:28—

Daniel 4:35—

Proverbs 16:9—

Mark 4:41—

God Is All Power

Revelation 19:6—

Psalms 62:11—

Genesis 18:14—

Revelation 1:8—

Isaiah 40:28-29—

Job 42:2—

Matthew 28:18—

John 10:27-30—

Luke 1:35-37—

Matthew 19:26—

God Is All Knowledge

1 John 3:20—

Isaiah 40:13-14—

Acts 15:18—

Isaiah 46:8-10—

Isaiah 66:18—

Psalms 147:4-5—

Psalms 50:10-11—

Jeremiah 23:24—

Psalms 139:1-5—

Proverbs 15:3—

God Is Everywhere Present

Jeremiah 23:23-24—

Proverbs 15:3—

Psalms 90:8—

Job 11:11—

1 Kings 8:27—

Psalms 139:7-10—

Matthew 28:19-20—

Hebrews 13:5-6—

Joshua 1:9—

Deuteronomy 31:6-8—

God Is Unchanging

Malachi 3:6—

James 1:17—

Psalms 102:25-27—

Hebrews 1:10-13—

Numbers 23:19—

1 Samuel 15:29—

Isaiah 46:9-10—

Isaiah 14:24—

Hebrews 6:13-19—

Hebrews 13:8—

God Is Holy

Revelation 15:4—

Exodus 15:11—

1 Samuel 2:2—

Psalms 145:17—

Isaiah 55:8-9—

Habakkuk 1:13—

Exodus 3:5—

Isaiah 6:1-5—

Psalms 30:4—

Luke 1:35—

God Is Love

1 John 4:7-8—

Jeremiah 31:3—

Lamentations 3:22-23—

Romans 8:35-39—

Romans 5:8—

Deuteronomy 7:7-8—

Ephesians 2:4-5—

John 3:16—

1 John 4:9-10—

1 John 4:19—

God Is Just

Psalms 97:1-2—

Deuteronomy 32:4—

Psalms 145:17—

Hosea 14:9—

Psalms 19:7-8—

Psalms 33:4—

Jeremiah 23:5-6—

1 John 2:1—

1 John 1:9—

Nehemiah 9:33—

God Is Good

Psalms 107:1—

Psalms 34:8—

Matthew 19:17—

Psalms 106:1—

Psalms 52:1—

Psalms 33:5—

Exodus 33:19—

Psalms 18:29—

Psalms 86:5—

Acts 10:38—

SCRIPTURE INDEX

189

190

BIBLE STUDY MATERIALS BY RICHARD BOOKER

BOOKS
For additional copies of this or other books by Richard Booker, order through your local bookstore or clip and mail the Order Form which is provided on the last page of this book following the tape list.

Richard's books can best be described as teaching books written in clear, easy-to-understand language and readable format for practical Christian living. They may be read or studied for deeper understanding of the Bible. They are primarily written for Christians of all levels of maturity but are appropriate for anyone seeking to know God. The following is a list of Richard's current books.

THE MIRACLE OF THE SCARLET THREAD
This book explains how the Old and New Testaments are woven together by the scarlet thread of the blood covenant to tell one complete story throughout the Bible.

COME AND DINE
This book takes the mystery and confusion out of the Bible. It provides background information on how we got the Bible, a survey of every book in the Bible and how each relates to Jesus Christ, practical principles, forms and guidelines for your own personal Bible study and a systematic plan for effectively reading, studying and understanding the Bible for yourself.

INTIMACY WITH GOD
This book is about the God of the Bible. It shows the ways in which God has revealed Himself to us and explains the attributes, plans and purposes of God. Then each attribute is related practically to the reader. This book takes you into the very heart of God and demonstrates how to draw near to Him.

BIBLE STUDY WORKSHOP

Richard developed and teaches a one-day workshop called *Come and Dine*. In this workshop, he teaches Christians how to study the Bible for themselves. Each participant receives a 95-page workbook which he or she will use as a lifetime Bible study reference aid. For a free brochure describing the workshop, check the appropriate box on the Order Form which is provided on the last page of this book following the tape list.

AUDIO CASSETTE TAPE ALBUMS

A list of Richard's teaching cassettes is included on the following pages. All tape series come in an attractive album for your convenience. To order tapes, check the appropriate box, then clip and mail the Order Form which is provided on the last page of this book following the tape list.

TAPE LIST

■ *The Bible Series*
BL1　Uniqueness Of The Bible
BL2　How The Books Became The Book
BL3　Survey of Old Testament
BL4　Survey of New Testament
BL5　How We Got Our English Bible
BL6　Getting Into The Bible
BL7　How To Study The Bible
BL8　How To Understand The Bible

■ *Getting To Know God—1*
KG1　Knowing God
KG2　The Self-Existing One
KG3　The Personal Spirit
KG4　The Trinity

■ *Getting To Know God—2*
KG1　God Is Sovereign
KG2　God Is All Power
KG3　God Is All Knowledge
KG4　God Is Everywhere Present
KG5　God Never Changes

■ *Getting To Know God—3*
KG1　God Is Holy
KG2　God Is Love
KG3　God Is Just
KG4　God Is Good

■ *Blood Covenant Series*
BC1　The Blood Covenant
BC2　What Was It Abraham Believed
BC3　The Tabernacle
BC4　The Sacrifices
BC5　The High Priest
BC6　The Passover

■ *Abundant Life Series*
AL1　Knowing Your Dominion
AL2　Identifying With Christ
AL3　Approprating His Lordship
AL4　Walking in the Spirit
AL5　Ministering in the Spirit
AL6　Wearing the Armor

■ *The Church Series*
CH1　The Church
CH2　The Body of Christ
CH3　Gifts of the Spirit
CH4　Equipping the Saints
CH5　Work of the Ministry
CH6　Building Up the Body

■ *Christian Family Series*
CF1　God's Purpose for Family
CF2　The Husband's Role
CF3　The Wife's Role
CF4　Parent & Children Roles

■ *Faith & Healing Series*
FH1　Divine Healing Today
FH2　Basis For Claiming Healing
FH3　Barriers To Healing

■ *End Time Series*
ET1　Coming World Events—1
ET2　Coming World Events—2
ET3　Judgment Of Christians
ET4　Seven-Year Tribulation
ET5　Second Coming Of Christ
ET6　Millennium
ET7　Great White Throne Judgment
ET8　New Heaven & New Earth

■ *The Feasts Series*
FE1　Passover
FE2　Unleavened Bread
FE3　Pentecost
FE4　Trumpets
FE5　Atonement
FE　Tabernacles

■ *Sacrifices Series*
SF1　Sin Offering
SF2　Trespass Offering
SF3　Burnt Offering
SF4　Meal Offering
SF5　Peace Offering

■ *Ephesians Series*

EP1	Background & Blessing
EP2	Prayer For Enlightenment
EP3	New Life In Christ
EP4	Who Is The Seed Of Abraham
EP5	Prayer For Enablement
EP6	Christian Unity
EP7	Ministering To The Saints
EP8	Ministry Of The Saints
EP9	Shedding The Graveclothes
EP10	Initating The Father
EP11	God's Order For Family
EP12	Spiritual Warfare

■ *Philippians Series*

PH1	Background & Prayer
PH2	Victory In Tribulation
PH3	Keys To Unity
PH4	Honoring One Another
PH5	True Righteousness
PH6	Going On With God
PH7	Standing Together
PH8	Sufficiency Of God

■ *Colossians Series*

CO1	Background
CO2	Person & Work Of Christ
CO3	Christ In You
CO4	Sufficiency Of Christ
CO5	Christ Our Life
CO6	New Man In Christ
CO7	Christ In The Home
CO8	Christ Outside The Home

■ *Thessalonians Series*

TH1	Background & Prayer
TH2	A Winning Defense
TH3	A Welcome Report
TH4	Walking to Please God
TH5	The Day of the Lord
TH6	Background & Prayer
TH7	Day of the Lord Again
TH8	No Bums Allowed

■ *Single Messages (Circle Below)*

SM1	Why God Had To Become man
SM2	Who Was That God Begat
SM3	Feasts Of The Lord
SM4	Philemon
SM5	Lord's Prayer
SM6	Handling Worry
SM7	Knowing God's Will
SM8	Spiritual Leprosy
SM9	Praying In The Name
SM10	Bible Baptisms
SM11	Signs Of His Coming
SM12	Times Of The Gentiles
SM13	Christian Giving
SM14	Master Theme Of Bible
SM15	The Dominant Force
SM16	Personal Testimony
SM17	Call To Discipleship
SM18	Where Are the Dead?